Business Guides on the Go

"Business Guides on the Go" presents cutting-edge insights from practice on particular topics within the fields of business, management, and finance. Written by practitioners and experts in a concise and accessible form the series provides professionals with a general understanding and a first practical approach to latest developments in business strategy, leadership, operations, HR management, innovation and technology management, marketing or digitalization. Students of business administration or management will also benefit from these practical guides for their future occupation/careers.

These Guides suit the needs of today's fast reader.

Jan Y. Yang

The Pricing Compass

Finding the Solution to Your Pricing Puzzle

Jan Y. Yang
Simon-Kucher & Partners
Frankfurt, Germany

ISSN 2731-4758   ISSN 2731-4766 (electronic)
Business Guides on the Go
ISBN 978-3-031-52059-4   ISBN 978-3-031-52060-0 (eBook)
https://doi.org/10.1007/978-3-031-52060-0

© The Editor(s) (if applicable) and The Author(s), under exclusive license to Springer Nature Switzerland AG 2024
This work is subject to copyright. All rights are solely and exclusively licensed by the Publisher, whether the whole or part of the material is concerned, specifically the rights of reprinting, reuse of illustrations, recitation, broadcasting, reproduction on microfilms or in any other physical way, and transmission or information storage and retrieval, electronic adaptation, computer software, or by similar or dissimilar methodology now known or hereafter developed.
The use of general descriptive names, registered names, trademarks, service marks, etc. in this publication does not imply, even in the absence of a specific statement, that such names are exempt from the relevant protective laws and regulations and therefore free for general use.
The publisher, the authors, and the editors are safe to assume that the advice and information in this book are believed to be true and accurate at the date of publication. Neither the publisher nor the authors or the editors give a warranty, expressed or implied, with respect to the material contained herein or for any errors or omissions that may have been made. The publisher remains neutral with regard to jurisdictional claims in published maps and institutional affiliations.

This Springer imprint is published by the registered company Springer Nature Switzerland AG
The registered company address is: Gewerbestrasse 11, 6330 Cham, Switzerland

Paper in this product is recyclable.

Preface

The Pricing Compass is a comprehensive guide to pricing strategies and tactics for product managers and pricing practitioners. It provides a pragmatic check on pricing maturity, addressing the reasons why pricing fails, what good pricing looks like, and how pricing concepts are applied.

This book covers a broad spectrum of pricing topics governing different stages of a business, including determining the starting point of the pricing journey, identifying unique selling propositions, disclosing willingness to pay (WTP), conducting effective customer profiling, improving promotions, and managing distribution from a pricing standpoint.

In addition, this book examines the importance of price increase campaigns, the woes of price wars, dynamic pricing, and behavioral pricing vs. value pricing. It also goes over the concept of price elasticity and how to navigate complex pricing situations.

Readers will find useful pricing tools and techniques in this book, such as the KANO model, the pricing sandbox, the ABCD analysis, systematic product categorization, and the promotion toolkit. By understanding the different aspects of pricing and implementing effective strategies, businesses of all stages can navigate the challenges of pricing and achieve sustainable success in today's competitive market.

There is a solution to every pricing puzzle!

Frankfurt, Germany   Jan Y. Yang

Contents

1	**Pricing Is Not What You Think**	1
1.1	Pricing Is Not Just About the Price	2
1.2	Strategic or Tactical	3
1.3	A Pragmatic Check on Pricing Maturity	4
1.4	Summary	6
2	**There Is a Solution to Every Pricing Puzzle**	7
2.1	When and Why Pricing Fails	7
	2.1.1 Ignorance	8
	2.1.2 Arrogance	9
	2.1.3 Imprudence	11
	2.1.4 Indecisiveness	13
2.2	What Does Good Pricing Look Like	16
2.3	What You Can Expect from the Next Chapters	18
2.4	Summary	19
3	**Let Us Get Started**	21
3.1	Define the Starting Point (Loop)	21
3.2	Discover Your Unique Selling Point (USP)	24
3.3	Reveal Willingness to Pay (WTP)	28
	3.3.1 The Pricing Sandbox	29

	3.3.2	van Westendorp	31
	3.3.3	Gabor Granger	35
	3.3.4	Conjoint Analysis	38
	3.3.5	Price Experiment	42
	3.3.6	Connecting the Dots	47
3.4	Price It!: The Moment of Truth (MoT)		50
3.5	Summary		51

4 Keep the Ball Rolling — 53

4.1	Understand Your Customers		55
4.2	Expand, Differentiate and Price Smartly		57
4.3	Build Fences Early on		61
	4.3.1	The Good	61
	4.3.2	The Bad	62
	4.3.3	The Ugly	63
	4.3.4	The Unsaid	64
4.4	Meet Price Elasticity		65
	4.4.1	The Concept	65
	4.4.2	The Relevance	66
	4.4.3	The Limitation	67
	4.4.4	The Application	69
4.5	Summary		73

5 Maneuver Shades of Pricing — 77

5.1	How to Navigate Complexity		77
	5.1.1	ABCD Analysis	78
	5.1.2	Systematic Product Categorization	80
5.2	How to Improve Promotions		83
	5.2.1	Who Is Eligible for Promotions	85
	5.2.2	What Products Are Suitable for Promotions	86
	5.2.3	How to Design Effective Promotions	89
5.3	How to Manage Distribution		94
	5.3.1	Is Distribution Outdated?	94
	5.3.2	Managing Distribution from a Pricing Perspective	96

		5.3.3	The GBB Pricing Model	98
		5.3.4	Price Model Transition	102
		5.3.5	Discounts or Rebates	103
	5.4	How to Increase Prices		105
		5.4.1	Rob's Price Increase Campaign: A Fictitious Case	105
		5.4.2	A Recapitulation	110
		5.4.3	The Sequel	112
		5.4.4	Last Remarks on Price Increase	113
	5.5	Stay Away from a Price War!		114
		5.5.1	Nobody Wins in the End	114
		5.5.2	Rethink Price War	116
	5.6	Dynamic Pricing		118
	5.7	Monetize the Predictable		119
		5.7.1	Behavioral Pricing vs. Value Pricing	119
		5.7.2	Four Behavioral Pricing Tricks	120
	5.8	Summary		125
6	**Embark on the Pricing Journey**			129
	6.1	Set Sail		130
	6.2	Navigate Rough Waters		131
	6.3	Sail to New Shores		133
	6.4	Per Astra Ad Astra		134
	6.5	Summary		135

References   137

Index   143

List of Figures

Fig. 2.1	Time value of pricing measures	15
Fig. 3.1	Product-market fit	23
Fig. 3.2	Product-market-price fit	23
Fig. 3.3	KANO model—basic idea	25
Fig. 3.4	KANO model—data generation	26
Fig. 3.5	KANO model—interpretation	27
Fig. 3.6	Pricing sandbox exercise	30
Fig. 3.7	Revenue and profit curve based on pricing sandbox	31
Fig. 3.8	Example of van Westendorp willingness-to-pay curves	33
Fig. 3.9	Example of a rearranged van Westendorp price-volume curve	34
Fig. 3.10	Conjoint trade-off mockup	39
Fig. 3.11	Example of utility curves	41
Fig. 3.12	Instafloss pricing options	45
Fig. 3.13	General pricing route	47
Fig. 4.1	From uniform price to differentiated price	58
Fig. 4.2	Price fencing	61
Fig. 4.3	Three different types of demand curves	68
Fig. 4.4	Price elasticity from historical data	70
Fig. 5.1	ABCD analysis	78
Fig. 5.2	Pricing by category	80
Fig. 5.3	Get the best of promotion—who?	85
Fig. 5.4	Get the best of promotion—what?	87
Fig. 5.5	Get the best of promotion—how?	93

Fig. 5.6   The relationship between purchase value and gross
            profit margin   97
Fig. 5.7   Distributer pricing journey—the GBB model   98
Fig. 5.8   Distributor price waterfall   102
Fig. 6.1   The three phases of a pricing journey   130

List of Tables

Table 1.1	Pricing maturity self-assessment	4
Table 1.2	Pricing maturity ratings	5
Table 3.1	Example of a Gabor Granger questionnaire	36
Table 3.2	Results of price test—milk shake	37
Table 3.3	Financial impact of price test—milk shake	37
Table 4.1	Repricing of a SaaS product	54
Table 4.2	Financial impact of price adjustments	71
Table 5.1	ABCD deep-dive	79
Table 5.2	Price engineering based on ABCD analysis	79
Table 5.3	Distributor discount matrix	100
Table 5.4	Rob's price increase campaign—starting situation	106
Table 5.5	Rob's price increase campaign—price increase target by customer category	107
Table 5.6	Rob's price increase campaign—price increase target by customer-product category	108

List of Equations[1]

Equation 4.1: Price elasticity   65
Equation 4.2: The product rule   66
Equation 4.3: The magic formula   67

---

[1] "Politics is for the present, but an equation is for eternity."—Albert Einstein

1

Pricing Is Not What You Think

Price is everywhere. However, people usually do not think about pricing until the moment that they are compelled to do so. Product managers and pricing practitioners, most of all, have the pleasure of pricing encounters.

So how to price it? Most likely, you might entertain thoughts such as:

Let us check how much others are charging for similar products.
If I want to make a profit, I will have to charge at least $250.
If the customer does not use my service, she would have to pay the other guy $50. Therefore, $40 should be a good deal for her.
Because the rent is much higher at the airport, a cup of cappuccino could cost 40% more.
What a hot day today! I can easily charge a 20% premium for the iced lemonade.
Our factory is running at capacity. We should raise the price by at least 10%.
I do not know how much it should sell for. Let us try $100 and see how it goes.
…

The list goes on.

All the abovementioned thoughts share one commonality that lies at the core of any pricing approach—i.e., a pricing decision is made relative to some sort of reference. The pricing reference would vary from case to case. It could be competition, cost, an alternative solution, location, time, or capacity utilization, as the statements above exemplify. In the worst case that you do not have any suitable reference to work with, you will have to create your own through a price experiment (see the last statement above: "*let us try $100*").

Putting a number to a product or service is not rocket science. The challenge that puzzles product managers, entrepreneurs, and other pricing practitioners has to do with how to find the *right* price.

From a pricing consultant's perspective, pricing is often a journey without a predefined roadmap. We may still arrive at the destination, by mere chance. However, there is a risk that we go astray or get stranded on that journey. It is human nature to shun uncertainties. Running an enterprise comes down to taking calculated risks while reducing uncertainty. A pricing compass is needed.

1.1 Pricing Is Not Just About the Price

Many of us do not understand that pricing is more than just finding a price. First, the concept of price per se can be misleading. The price does not exist. In fact, the concept of price is profound and multidimensional. Although you may not realize it right away, a plethora of elements constitute the so-called price: price tags, promotions, discounts, rebates, exclusive offers, coupons, surcharges, and even taxes. Price is a universe in its own right.

The final bill you pay in the end may deviate significantly from what is written on the price tag, depending on which elements mentioned above come into play and what kind of role they assume.

In this light, pricing would mean a process to identify the price elements that lead to the net price that a customer would ultimately pay in exchange for what they want. This sounds about right but is not complete yet.

In fact, the word "pricing" is a misnomer, as it only tells the half of the story.

Two thousand years ago, an ancient Roman would refer to both price and value as "*pretium*" (Simon, 2015). From a semantic standpoint, the Chinese characters for price (*Jia Ge*) and value (*Jia Zhi*) are likewise strikingly similar. If price and value are so entangled, then pricing should relate not only to finding price but also to finding value. Price and value are two sides of the same coin.

1.2 Strategic or Tactical

The word pricing suggests that pricing tackles price. In fact, to achieve a decent price, you need to have an in-depth understanding of what your customer values and how you fulfill that demand (how well relative to your competition, to be precise). In this sense, pricing should be both strategic (concerning value proposition and creation) and tactical (concerning value extraction).

I recall numerous meetings with my clients who asserted that pricing was tactical and functional. In fact, not all companies have a dedicated pricing function, especially small- and medium-sized companies. I have been trying hard to preach that pricing is of strategic importance, as it deals with value management and strategic positioning in essence. Admittedly, I often fail.

Over the years, I have seen business owners and management teams fall short to recognize the importance of pricing until they have paid a high price for their ignorance. The CEO of an irrigation equipment manufacturer shared with me the following story.

> Our company designs and manufactures high-end irrigation equipment. It was two years ago when the competition became so heated that I felt forced to fight back. Therefore, I made the call to cut the prices by 20%. It did not pan out well for us. It is a decision that I regret to date.
>
> What happened after the price reduction was a nightmare. Our staff slacked off, as they thought it was legitimate to make compromises following the price cut. As a result, complaints about product and service quality piled up swiftly, while sales remained sluggish. In the end, the pricing decision left us with disgruntled customers, reputational damage, and much less profits.

To make things even worse, we have not been able to reinstall the original price level since then. The price cut turned out to be an ugly scar. I swear that I will never do it again.

1.3 A Pragmatic Check on Pricing Maturity

Is there an uncomplicated way to tell whether a company is good at pricing? Yes, we can assess the pricing maturity of a company by using a set of indicators. I include a pragmatic checklist (see Table 1.1) so that the readers can perform a quick self-assessment by themselves.

It works as follows: for each statement that is true, you receive one point; if it is partially true, you have null; should one statement do not apply to

Table 1.1 Pricing maturity self-assessment

#	Do the following statements apply to your firm?	True (1)	Partially true (0)	False (–1)
1	Price positioning is clearly defined with reference to the corporate strategy			
2	Price image perceived by customers is line with target price positioning			
3	You do not base your pricing decisions purely on cost or competition			
4	Customers' use cases are clearly understood and serve as the foundation for product development			
5	Price (value) drivers are identified and serve as the foundation for product differentiation			
6	You conduct market research and data analysis on a regular basis to gain customer insights			
7	You understand the importance of pricing to your company's financial results			
8	You do the math based on price elasticity			
9	You have a Plan B should a pricing decision go wrong			
10	You regularly monitor pricing performance and take action as needed			
11	There is a clear pricing process in place, as well as defined roles and responsibilities			
12	All else being equal, the sales and pricing team is incentivized to achieve higher prices			

your company at all, one point will be subtracted accordingly. The total score will give you a sense of how good your company is at pricing.

As a rule of thumb, pricing maturity can be classified into five categories (see Table 1.2). Check out how well your company fares. Experience shows that assessments from distinct functions within one company could vary by a wide margin.

The description of the statements in the checklist should be self-explanatory. Nonetheless, I figure that it is necessary to elaborate on the terminology *price driver*, which is interchangeable with *value driver* in this book. I use the latter in the following example.

During the Q&A session of a pricing training, a participant sought advice on how to defend their prices in the face of intensifying competition.

> He: "I think we deserve a higher price than competitors because we offer much better service."
> I: "Fair enough. Please elaborate a bit more on what you mean by 'better.'"

This is the moment when he started stuttering. Finally, he summarized:

> "We have got more service staff."
> I: "Good to know. But so what? How does it benefit your customers? Can you quantify the benefit in a way?"

Table 1.2 Pricing maturity ratings

Total score	Classification	Description
>10	★★★★★	Excellent
(8 – 10]	★★★★	Good
(6 – 8]	★★★	Average
(4 – 6]	★★	Poor
≤4	★	Very poor

The conversation went on for a couple of more rounds before he sat down quietly (sadly).

My last piece of advice for him was to rethink whether he really needed to keep such a large service staff.

Now what does this episode above have to do with *value drivers*?

Well, value drivers are like building blocks of a Lego set. You need to pick the right ones to do it right—that is according to the manual in the box. Analogically, each of your customers would have their own idea of what their ideal product should comprise—a kind of manual.

A competent product manager would not build the Lego the way she or he feels like. Instead, they strive to discover the manual first, finding the right value drivers, and then start building the actual thing.

Beware that value drivers govern the entire user experience and thus are not limited to physical attributes. For example, value drivers of an electric vehicle could include brand, range, horsepower, exterior and interior design, in-cabin equipment, infotainment, autonomous driving, customer service, warranty, etc. Register the concept of value drivers. We will revisit it in the following chapters.

1.4 Summary

- The concept of price is profound and multidimensional.
- Price and value are two sides of the same coin.
- To achieve a decent price, you need to have an in-depth understanding of what your customer values and how well you fulfill that demand relative to your competition.
- Pricing should be both strategic (concerning value proposition and creation) and tactical (concerning value extraction).
- Pricing maturity assessment (Table 1.1) helps you assess the pricing maturity of your company.

2

There Is a Solution to Every Pricing Puzzle

Pricing is a puzzle. Many companies struggle with pricing decisions; others try to do something without knowing what is right for them; and many more wonder what happened only when bad pricing decisions backfired.

Before we continue, we need to define what a pricing failure is.

> **Pricing Failure Definition**
> Obtaining suboptimal results (e.g., revenue, profit, market share) as a result of a poor pricing decision.

2.1 When and Why Pricing Fails

Compared to other business functions, pricing has one distinctive disadvantage, namely, that the outcome of pricing work is subject to many *unknowns*:

How would customers react?
How would competitors react?
How would our own sales team react?
How would our cost structure change over the next year?

How would the macroeconomy develop in the next 24 months?
The list of questions goes on…

In the face of so many open questions, the complexity and uncertainty around pricing speaks volumes. The ultimate question for a business is to be or not to be at the mercy of the invisible hand. For the very reason that pricing is an intricate mechanism, exceptional care needs to be taken. There is no panacea for all pricing ills. As in treatment of all human diseases, the root cause needs to be found at the first step.

According to my observation, there are four capital sins that lead to pricing failures.

2.1.1 Ignorance

Symptoms:

- *The pricing function is nonexistent.*
- *"We follow the market price."*
- *"The price is determined by the cost."*

Pricing is not understood or misunderstood. Price is not actively managed because the management believes that price need not to be managed. Ignorant managers resort to two main sources when determining the price.

The first is the so-called market price. Market price is a basic economic concept and refers to the price at which assets, products, and services are bought and sold. It is determined considering the rate at which the product is demanded and supplied. In short, it shows the affordability level of customers, reflecting the cost they are ready to pay for their purchases, which increases or decreases the demand for the same in the marketplace (Wallstreetmojo Team, 2023). Nice and neat. However, as with all other economic concepts, managers need to enjoy it with a pinch of salt in the real world.

First, the market price is ephemeral. In perfect competition, supply and demand change constantly, while the market price changes over time. It is difficult to peg to something that is constantly changing; in less perfect competition, each supplier has sort of uniqueness to offer, eventually translating into a price advantage.

Second, we tend to find quasi-market prices in commodities markets, in which there is trivial difference in the products or services being offered. Commodity is, however, a management failure. There is always a way to differentiate from competitors. If one succeeds in product differentiation, then they ought to define their own market price, as a new market niche is born.

Costing information is the second main source that businesses use to determine the price. In fact, cost-plus pricing prevails at numerous companies, especially manufacturing companies, where costing information is readily available. Rules of thumb are frequently applied—so statements are circulating around like:

> 8–10 times cost is way to go in premium apparel business.
> 25% margin is the industry norm.
> We make a profit as long as we can cover the cost.

The popularity of cost-plus pricing is understandable because costs appear tangible. However, it just gives you a false sense of security. Costs are of a matter of fact, nothing more, nothing less. *Costs* are a valid reference for making pricing decisions. The challenge in cost-plus pricing lies in how to find the right *Plus*, which cost-plus pricing proponents often ignore or downplay.

2.1.2 Arrogance

Symptoms:

- *The pricing function exists but lacks substance.*
- *"We know all pricing drills."*
- *"We have read all pricing literature that is available on the market."*

While ignorance implies not knowing what you do not know, arrogance means not knowing what you know. The latter tends to do more harm.

Arrogant clients are difficult to work with. They often claim to have a pricing function in place and act according to the book (not this book unfortunately). In most situations, the pricing function is often far from functioning.

As mentioned earlier, pricing resembles an intricate mechanism, very much as in a mechanical watch. For it to work properly, the mainspring must be wound periodically; the clockwork needs to be cleansed and calibrated once a while. Analogically, pricing competence is not meant to be built for good; pricing muscles need to be trained regularly to stay in a decent shape. Arrogance guarantees a foreseeable shelf time of pricing capability whose substance erodes with the elapse of time.

It is, therefore, a big red flag when someone claims that their company knows everything about pricing and does everything about right, even though there is a slim chance that it might be true.

The other day, I was chatting with a client about the application of conjoint analysis in an upcoming market research for them. Briefly, conjoint analysis works by asking customers to rate varied product concepts. When a company understands how its customers value its products or services' features, it can use these insights to develop its pricing strategy (Stobierski, 2020). Conjoint is an intricate exercise and belongs to my favorite pricing topics. I usually have an enjoyable time exchanging ideas with practitioners on conjoint. However, this conversation turned out to be somehow different.

The gentleman at the other side of the table was CMO at a promising mobility startup. He genuinely showed no interest in what kind of conjoint work we did. In the meantime, he asserted that his team did already whatever we had to offer. Well, as the proverb goes, you can lead a horse to water, but you cannot make him drink. Nothing is left to be said. At that time, I would not know that the rising star would file for bankruptcy within the next 24 months. I could have known better.

Another form of arrogance manifests itself in the deceptive notion of pricing literacy. The CEO of a multi-billion-dollar company took pride in having his pricing team familiarize themselves with all pricing books available on the market. I had the chance to take a peep at the reading notes which summarized all pricing frameworks including some of mine. On the one hand, I felt flattered; on the other hand, I felt irritated—it would be too easy to learn a trade by just reading!

Later, I got to learn the head of pricing at that company, who confided her dilemma to me: the more she reads up on the pricing subject, the more she tends to disagree with the CEO on how pricing should be managed at their company. One of their recent conversations went like this:

> She: "Value-based pricing is the way to go. All leading companies in our industry apply a sort of value-based pricing."
> He: "Well noted. I fully support value-based pricing. However, I just do not think whether it is the right moment for us to switch to value-based pricing, considering we are facing such heated competition at the present. Let us stick to competition-driven pricing for now."
> She: "Hm… fine. However, how do we should we set the price relative to competition?"
> He: "Good question! It is exactly your job to figure it out."
>
> She was like… *"How can I?"*

I can tell she is clearly overwhelmed. However, if the big boss is not buying (investing) into it, what can she do? I do feel for her.

Arrogance is so deadly!

2.1.3 Imprudence

Symptoms:

- *CEO is CPO.*
- *"Pricing is in line with our brand positioning."*
- *"The price could be $10 lower or higher."*

If you have not heard of CPO, it means Chief Pricing Officer. Few organizations have this position dedicated to pricing on the executive management team. We revisit the topic in greater detail in Chap. 6. For now, it suffices to know that it is usually a blessing that the CEO (Chief

Executive Officer) at a company assumes the role of CPO. This means that pricing has received due attention from top management. However, there is also an unwanted side effect—pricing is "stuck" on a strategical level, i.e., without digging into the nitty-gritty details—which can have an enormous impact on the pricing outcome.

We have learned that pricing is both strategic and tactical. A CEO is charged with steering the company strategically. In this role, CEOs will/ should not have time to take care of the operational side of pricing. The moment they falsely believe that they have full control over pricing, pricing will get out of hand.

Statements such as *"Pricing is in line with our brand positioning"* are right and important, speaking to the artistic nature of pricing. In addition, pricing must be as analytical and quantitative as possible. At the end of the day, a number needs to be determined. A price ballpark is good to know. However, it is a job unfinished.

The CEO of a cosmetic company once introduced to me his so-called pricing approach 2.0 with great enthusiasm. His company used to apply cost-plus pricing. In a casual chat previously, I explained to him the drawbacks of cost-plus pricing and exchanged a few thoughts on how to make better pricing decisions. Obviously, he took my advice to heart. By the way, he is an uncrowned CPO at his company. The executive committee will convene about pricing-related topics. In the end, it is he who makes all the pricing decisions.

Now without further due, let me explain what is his pricing approach 2.0. Under the premise that his brand is a leading brand in its market niche, their products can be priced in the same league as prestigious imported brands. Thus far so good. He went on:

> We have this new generation of product coming up, which has four times the volume of one effective ingredient compared to a similar product from a renowned French brand. We had already decided to price it at $498, which is lower than the French brand but will yield a decent margin. We were all wonderfully comfortable with it.

I wanted to ask him what a decent margin is, but I did not want to interrupt him. He continued:

I realized that there was untapped price potential after listening to you the other day. I managed to convince the management team and the board of directors and raised the retail price to $598 in the last minute. We ended up with a price higher than our competitive benchmark, which was an unprecedented move in our company's history. The board was very skeptical, to say the least.

It has been a couple of months since the product launch. The sales reports came in as expected. Thanks to your advice, we have made at least $5 million more in revenue and profit!

What a pleasant surprise! I was amazed at the speed that he moved things around/forward and wished I could partake in the success financially. Joke aside, I was happy that he took my indirect advice—I did not recommend a $100 price adjustment after all. I could not either. More information and analysis would be required to make a pricing recommendation.

On the one hand, I can understand that he had to act fast to stick to the original launch plan; on the other hand, I fear that the pricing approach 2.0 that he proudly presented will not entail any analytical components in the future either.

I attempted to urge him to think about how much more value the "overperformance" in that effective ingredient would bring to customers. The resulting value-added should determine the product's "*premiumness*." Instead of $5 million, he could have made an extra $10 million. I do not believe I succeeded in the end. He appeared to be quite content with the $5 million pricing windfall.

2.1.4 Indecisiveness

Symptoms:

- *Nobody makes the call.*
- *"What if competitors follow suit?"*
- *"What if we missed the sales target?"*

The plan is silver, and the action is golden. All good pricing decisions need to be implemented. The last sin of pricing is indecisiveness, or the lack of determination to take actions.

Some leaders make a move as soon as they make up their minds. I like speed demons whole-heartedly. Pricing consultants or any consultants are enablers, as we only analyze and make suggestions. Good clients are doers who make suggestions come true. The CEO of the abovementioned cosmetic company is a case in point. Without doers our work is worthless, and we are valueless.

I also have a fond memory of the CEO of a SaaS[1] company. We were in the middle of a price optimization project, for which he was the main sponsor. In the interim report readout, we pointed out a profit leakage caused by some legacy pricing issues. That meeting went well. Everybody left the conference room with a happy face.

The next day I bumped into the CEO in the hallway. He saluted me and casually mentioned that he had instructed the IT department to resolve the pricing issues we identified. In addition, it was done as we spoke. I was shocked:

> Did you just do that?
> Why not? Your analysis made sense to me. You also showed us that the potential risks were limited. I do not see any reason to procrastinate.
> Me on the inside: "well done…"

So here is the thing. In most cases, a price adjustment is not risk-free. Nevertheless, the size of the risk can be calculated or simulated in different scenarios, as best-in-class companies routinely do. If the benefit outweighs the risk, it will be only rational to go for it. We should keep in mind the time value of pricing measures (see Fig. 2.1).

The time window of pricing measures comes and goes. Unless you have pricing superpower, there are two and only two right moments to touch upon pricing. The first is when you launch a new product to the market; the second is when something new comes into play—be it an upgrade of your own product, a new competitor's product, change in

---

[1] SaaS: software as a service

2 There Is a Solution to Every Pricing Puzzle

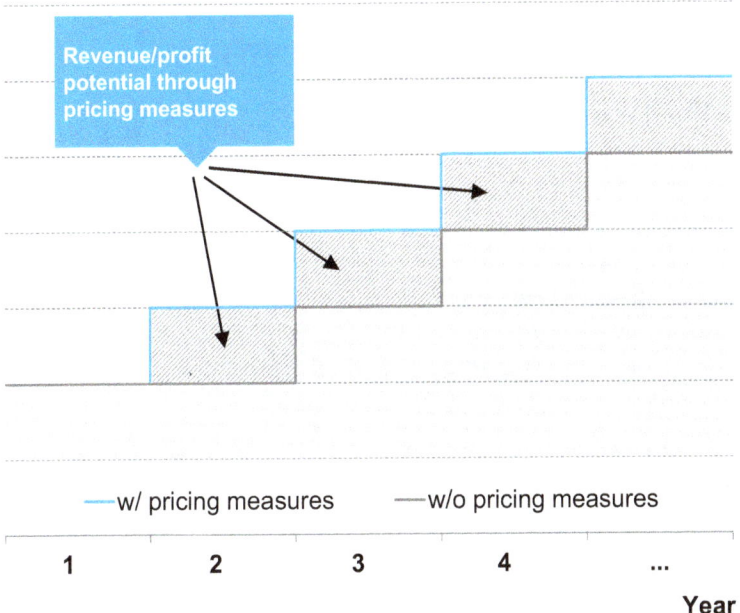

Fig. 2.1 Time value of pricing measures

customers' sentiment, etc. In both situations, time is precious good. If a time window of pricing measures is missed, the lost revenue/profit potential will never be recouped.

The cure for the last sin "indecisiveness" is exceptionally obvious—look at the numbers—numbers do not cheat. There is no return without risk.

In sum, I cannot decide which sin is the worst of all. They are all bad and harmful. In contrast, what does good pricing look like?

2.2 What Does Good Pricing Look Like

There are a few signs that bode well for good pricing.

1. **Good pricing starts from the top.**

   We often say that pricing belongs to the board room, by which we mean that top management should make it clear that pricing is of strategic importance and must be treated seriously.

   The leaders should have in-depth knowledge about the relevance of pricing for the financial results of the company. Good leaders are unambiguous and talk numbers. They can tell you immediately how a 10% price increase or decrease would impact their business. This is the kind of pricing leadership that we need.

2. **Good pricing is teamwork.**

   Pricing permeates every corner of the organization. It takes a team to make pricing work; different minds across departments must work together and bring in perspectives and know-how.

   Pricing belongs to the board room. For management to make informed decisions, the pricing team must have proper preparation of numbers and insights—the marketing facts, so to speak.

   The marketing facts are twofold. On the inside, they would include product specs, price history, costing information, sales targets, etc.; on the outside, they would include information on competitors' products, costs, pricing, and sales strategy and insights into customers' preferences and purchase behavior, etc. As you can see, information must be collected from different stakeholders. The process can be time-consuming and messy. The pricing leader at a company will have to be a good networker. Otherwise, it will not fly.

3. **Good pricing is thorough.**

   As previously stated, good pricing necessitates marketing facts. The more knowledge you have, the more probable it is that you will make an informed conclusion.

The quality of pricing decisions improves significantly if you can acquire data from various sources to gain more reference points. Pricing managers with experience use a wealth of information in their work. By information, I mean not just the abovementioned marketing facts, but also the expectations (and, at times, agendas) of internal and external stakeholders.

A sophisticated pricing team would go even one step further and run simulations to have a better understanding of different pricing scenarios. Knowing what might come your way is the best way to protect yourself from unexpected surprises.

4. **Good pricing becomes better over time.**

Pricing is complex work. The profession has come a long way but is still far from mature. The pricing team at any organization needs to evolve to stay abreast of latest trends—from a market point of view and technologically speaking.

The market is changing at a fast pace. Digitalization is taking the market by storm. Consumers' sentiment is increasingly difficult to fathom. Competitors are becoming increasingly sophisticated in marketing and sales besides other functions. All these trends pose challenges to pricing and necessitate constant adaptations in mindsets and renewal of skillsets.

In recent years, advanced technologies such as AI,[2] neuroscience, and various analytical methods have made inroads into pricing. There are thousands of ways to make better pricing decisions, thanks to technological advancement. Imagination is the only limit.

I have seen startups with a total staff of 10 using in-house developed BI[3] and software to tackle pricing challenges; I have also seen Fortune 500 companies with a central pricing team of 20 people indulge themselves in spreadsheets (of different versions, of course)—not to mention that many values in the spreadsheets are hard-wired—do not get me started.

Good pricing needs to get better to stay good over time.

---

[2] AI: artificial intelligence
[3] BI: business intelligence

2.3 What You Can Expect from the Next Chapters

This book is not meant to be an all-encompassing textbook heavy on science and theory. Instead, I want to provide product managers and pricing practitioners with essential knowledge about how to get their job done at various stages of the business. Along the way, I will share real stories, best practices, useful tools, and lastly my personal reflections.

Admittedly, different industries face different pricing challenges. There is no way that I can sort out all these nuances across industries. Nevertheless, I will try to cover pricing tasks common for both the B2C and B2B sectors. Some pricing challenges may appear different on the surface; in essence, the same pricing principles should still apply.

Readers with prior knowledge about pricing would know that there are three prevailing pricing methods, i.e., cost-plus, competition-driven, and value-based. I have intentionally refrained from using this kind of classification for a simple reason: no one uses only one method in practice. I have explained why in Sect. 2.2 and will touch upon this topic again in some other chapters.

The rest of the book is organized as follows. Readers can jump to the respective chapters, depending on their circumstances and interest.

Chapter 3 discusses how to kickstart pricing from scratch. It is most interesting for startups that try to gain a foothold in the market or established companies that are about a launch a new product.

Chapter 4 centers on pricing past the fledgling stage, where the business has established itself and customers' needs start to diversify. Pricing is growing in complexity parallel to sales growth.

Chapter 5 delves into the details of price management of a more mature company and addresses topics such as complexity management, promotions, distribution pricing, price maintenance, price wars, dynamic pricing, and lastly the "inexplicable" side of human beings and its implications for pricing.

Chapter 6 sheds light behind the curtains, taking the readers on the pricing journey in a time machine. We will review the milestones of the pricing journey and the evolution of roles and responsibilities of the pricing crew along the way.

2.4 Summary

- Compared to other business functions, pricing has one distinctive disadvantage, namely, that the outcome of pricing work is subject to many unknowns.
- There are four capital sins that lead to pricing failures.

  - **Ignorance**
  Price is not actively managed because the management believes that price need not to be managed.
  - **Arrogance**
  Pricing muscles need to be trained regularly to stay in a decent shape. Arrogance guarantees a foreseeable shelf time of pricing capability whose substance erodes over time.
  - **Imprudence**
  The moment a CEO falsely believes that they have full control over pricing, pricing will get out of hand.
  - **Indecisiveness**
  The plan is silver, and the action is golden. If a time window of pricing measures is missed, the lost revenue/profit potential will never be recouped.

- There are a few signs that bode well for good pricing. Good pricing …

  - … starts from the top.
  - … is teamwork.
  - … is thorough.
  - … becomes better over time.

3

Let Us Get Started

3.1 Define the Starting Point (Loop)

Peter Drucker had a clear message for business owners (Hoover, 2022):

> "There is only one definition of business purpose: to create a customer"
>
> - Peter Drucker

In his 2017 Letter to Shareholders, Jeff Bezos called out the underlying nature of customers' ever-increasing expectations. "One thing I love about customers," Jeff wrote, "is that they are divinely discontent…People have a voracious appetite for a better way, and yesterday's 'wow' quickly becomes today's 'ordinary'" (Slater, 2023).

What can we learn from these two great minds?

(a) Customers are critical for a business.
(b) Customers are difficult to please.

It follows that the success of a business lies in customer-centricity. However, customer-centricity does not mean to fulfill every need of customers at any cost. Hermann Simon asserts in his book "True Profit!" (Simon, 2021):

> "Profits are the cost of survival and the creators of new value"
>
> - Hermann Simon

Businesses must turn a profit to live up to their purpose. Value creation must be rewarded to finance innovations on a sustainable basis. This is a fundamental challenge that confronts any great innovative idea.

The prevailing notion of a successful business at the fledgling stage is usually associated with the so-called product-market fit. It says that you need to find and fill a void in the market when starting out. See Fig. 3.1.

However, product-market fit would not guarantee a successful business case. Filling a void only makes sense when you get paid adequately from a business point of view. Whether you get paid comes down to uniqueness. You become unique either because you resolve a problem that nobody else can or because you can resolve it in a more cost-effective way. The ultimate measure of the real product-market fit is price. As a result, product-market fit only makes sense when there is also a product-market-price fit. See Fig. 3.2.

Focusing merely on product-market fit risks falling into an innovation trap and resulting in wasted investment and dissatisfied customers. Adding price to the equation puts customer's value perception to the test, as they reveal their willingness to pay for the new product being

Fig. 3.1 Product-market fit

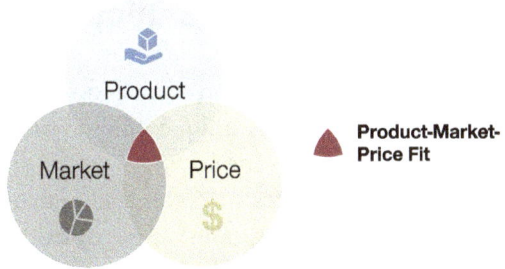

Fig. 3.2 Product-market-price fit

conceived. The gain (value) must be at least as great as sacrifice (price), which is critical for any healthy relationship, including the one between the company and the customer.

The starting point of a viable business must lie with the customer. To be more precise, product managers need to know what problem they are going to solve for the customer—be it disruptive (something completely new) or incremental (something more cost-effective).

It will be a loop, as the value creation journey also ends with the customer. Whether it will be a happy ending depends on how much the customer is willing to pay for what she/he receives. An innovation that no one is going to buy or afford is a failed endeavor and waste of energy. When there is no product-market-price fit, the product manager must start over and find something fresh.

In sum, customer-centricity plays a vital role in businesses' survival. The journey begins with the customer, who appreciates the solution to her/his problem. The ultimate yardstick of the appreciation is the price, which determines how long the journey will last.

Starting out from and building on customers' unmet needs is an ideal situation. In many cases, product managers may first develop a cool idea that they think might fulfill a need, which is totally fine. However, the sooner the better, they should loop in the customer perspective and think of the product-market-price fit! Remember what customers like to talk about is value, what they believe is the price that they pay. We want to make them walk the talk.

3.2 Discover Your Unique Selling Point (USP)

Unique selling point sounds unique and cool. However, the problem is that uniqueness often lacks proof. A unique selling point does not hold unless customers are willing to pay for it.

Before we talk about techniques to reveal willingness to pay, let us revisit what makes a unique selling point. Also called a unique selling proposition, unique selling point (USP) is a marketing statement that differentiates a product or brand from its competitors. A USP is superlative and might be built on the lowest cost, the highest quality, the most unforgettable experience, the first in its product class or another trait that sets the offering apart from the competition. A unique selling point can be thought of as "what you have that competitors do not" (Sheldon, 2022).

A USP does not come out of the blue. It needs to be engineered in most cases, where the KANO model could come in handy. The KANO model is named after Noriaki Kano, who invented the model as a theory for product development and customer satisfaction in the 1980s. The basic idea is illustrated in Fig. 3.3.

A product manager is often concerned about what kind of features should be included in a new product. Kano theorizes that there are five categories of product features that come into consideration (Wikipedia, 2023e).

- **Must-have**
- These are the features that customers take for granted. When done well, customers are just neutral; however, when done poorly, customers will be very dissatisfied.

Fig. 3.3 KANO model—basic idea

- *Example*: wheels of a passenger car
- **Expected**
- These features result in satisfaction when fulfilled and dissatisfaction when not fulfilled. Competition usually centers around these features.
- *Example*: size and juiciness of a hamburger patty
- **Excitement**
- These features provide an elevated level of satisfaction when provided, however, do not cause dissatisfaction when not fulfilled. These are unexpected aspects that contribute to the *wow* factor. A USP is to be found in the excitement features!
- *Example*: touchscreen of the first-generation iPhone
- **Indifferent**
- These features do not result in either customer satisfaction or customer dissatisfaction. They are usually hidden to the eyes of customers.
- *Example*: fuel consumption of an airplane (for most people)
- **Killers**
- Customers dislike these features, hence including them will result in lower consumer satisfaction and should be avoided. Killers are especially vicious when customers must pay for them.
- *Example*: excessive packaging of an ordinary product

The terminology of the KANO features has been evolving since its inception, however, the essence of which has remained intact. Product managers must have a sharp vision about the "*Must-have*" and "*Expected*" features and avoid "*Killers*" of any kind.

The operationalization of the KANO model is straightforward if you can survey the potential customers directly. Although you also create a KANO model based on the judgment of your own team, it is highly recommendable to include an external survey. The larger the sample size is, the more robust the results. As a rule of thumb, you should at least have 30 respondents of a homogenous customer group. There are only two questions per feature to be asked to generate the data needed for the KANO analysis. Check out Fig. 3.4.

At the first step, you just need to ask two questions for each feature you have in mind, where the scale of answers is the same, ranging from "dislike" to "like" in five steps, the only difference in the questions being whether a specific feature is present or not. Make sure the feature description is clear, especially if the survey is conducted online.

Now, taking the responses from a sample of potential customers, you will be able to classify the tested features at Step 2, where you see how the five categories of features mentioned above emerge. A sixth category named "Question mark" contains the features that do not fall into the other five categories due to a lack of consensus among the respondents. Usually, they can be disregarded for further analysis.

Step 1: Question: be or not to be?

What is your reaction… If	I like it	I expect it	I am neutral	I can live with it	I dislike it
"Feature" is present					
"Feature" is NOT present					

Step 2: Classification

		Feature NOT present				
		I like it	I expect it	I am neutral	I can live with it	I dislike it
Feature present	I like it	Question mark	Excitement	Excitement	Excitement	Expected
	I expect it	Killer	Indifferent	Indifferent	Indifferent	Must-have
	I am neutral	Killer	Indifferent	Indifferent	Indifferent	Must-have
	I can live with it	Killer	Indifferent	Indifferent	Indifferent	Must-have
	I dislike it	Killer	Killer	Killer	Killer	Question mark

Fig. 3.4 KANO model—data generation

Applying a discrete analysis method, you could assign each tested feature to one of the five categories, depending on the opinion of most participants. An alternative way, which I prefer, is to perform a continuous analysis, in which you take the nuances in preferences into account. Specifically, you do not depict the preferences in black and white, acknowledging the existence of gray zones. Figure 3.5 gives you an idea of how the results of a continuous analysis look like.

Usually, respondents do not unanimously assign a feature to a certain category. Visualization with the help of a matrix can give us a good overview of the dispersion of customer preferences. To achieve this, we recode the answers with scores between –2 and 4 (for the functional question: I like it (4), I expect it (2), I am neutral (0), I can tolerate it (–1), I dislike it (–2); for the dysfunctional question: I like it (–2), I expect it (–1), I am neutral (0), I can tolerate it (2), I dislike it (4)). See the table in Fig. 3.5. Using this method, you can assign an exact value to every feature for every respondent you surveyed. As a next step, it is possible to calculate a mean value across all respondents that can, in turn, be entered into a continuous KANO graph (Pfeifer, 2019).

A word of warning: using means or medians would average out individual preferences. Look at the standard deviations or a histogram of the individual values to gain a sense of the sampling distribution. You might

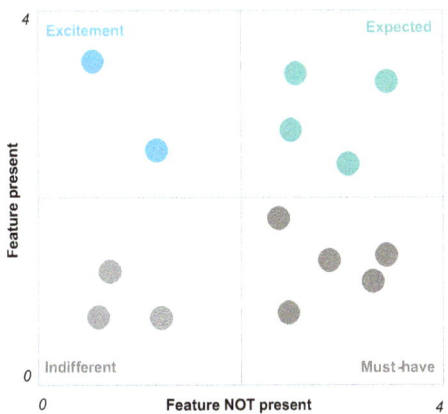

Fig. 3.5 KANO model—interpretation

also want to compute the coefficient of variation[1] to that end. Too large a variation means that you have customer groups with distinct preferences within the sample. If it is the case, you should consider slicing the data and focusing on one of the customer groups at the first step, where you would have a competitive edge.

After all data cleansing and crunching has been completed, it is time to decide which excitement feature will make your USP. There are two factors that should be considered. The first factor is your ability to provide that feature in a cost-effective way. It is fitting to conduct a cost–benefit analysis to evaluate whether the intended USP is financially viable. The second factor is the ability of your (potential) competitors to mimic your USP. A USP must be hard to emulate; otherwise, it will not be unique for a long time.

3.3   Reveal Willingness to Pay (WTP)

Now it is time to talk about willingness to pay (WTP). It is bread and butter of any product manager or pricing practitioner. It plays an essential role in how you price your product. It is also a tricky one.

On the one hand, it is often a dilemma for the decision maker: should I price high to suit the value that I offer, or should I price low to make sure that I reach critical mass to be relevant? It is a choice that must be made. In this context, WTP should never be treated as a stand-alone topic. Instead, the real question we want to resolve is how much sales we generate and at which price level. In other words, we need to reveal the demand curve that elucidates the relationship between price and demand/sales volume.

On the other hand, customers may not be willing to disclose their true willingness to pay, or they may not be able to tell their willingness to pay, especially in the case of new products for which they lack a prior reference. It is almost impossible to pinpoint the willingness to pay of any

---

[1] The coefficient of variation (CV) is defined as the ratio of the standard deviation σ to the mean μ. The higher the coefficient of variation, the greater the level of dispersion around the mean.

individual. In fact, human beings are not particularly good at articulating their needs.

In the meantime, product managers and pricing practitioners should be more interested in the aggregate willingness to pay of a certain customer group or any meaningful subgroup of the customer base because we want to understand how much sales volume we will be able to generate.

There are a few techniques that we can apply to determine WTP and the underlying demand curves. Some of them require only simple calculations, while others involve more complex analyses. We will go through all of them in greater detail in what follows.

3.3.1 The Pricing Sandbox

One of the most straightforward ways to obtain WTP is to directly solicit expert opinions. The so-called pricing sandbox is conducted in a structured workshop format to that effect. Simply put, a group of experts sit together and estimate volume development according to different price scenarios. The process consists of individual assessments followed up by group discussion to reach an agreement on most likely outcomes in the end. The name sandbox is a tribute to the underlying "*trial-and-error*" principle. Although it may sound a bit unserious/unreal, the pricing sandbox method has proven to work out well in the past. It should be noted that a few prerequisites must be met.

First, you need real experts who are knowledgeable about the product and the target market. Second, they must voice their opinions openly and honestly. In this regard, having an experienced moderator to run the workshop will be immensely helpful. Third, the background information on the underlying product including needed assumptions about the market should be shared before the exercise starts. Finally, opinions should be backed up by facts and numbers, whenever possible.

The exercise of pricing sandbox per se is uncomplicated: participants are asked to estimate volumes (either indexed or real numbers) along a predefined price range. Please note that we should focus on obtaining the relative volume changes at different price points. We can determine the exact volume at a later stage.

The price points can also be indexed, with the starting point set to 100. The starting point corresponds to the base scenario volume. That said, I prefer to work with actual price points, which are usually easier for the participants to relate to. A visualization of the exercise can be seen in Fig. 3.6.

As indicated earlier, each participant should complete her, or his volume estimates individually before comparing and discussing the results in the group. To ensure a holistic view, it is important to invite stakeholders from different departments to participate in the workshop.

It is likely that the individual estimates diverge at certain price points. The moderator should encourage the outliers to elaborate on their rationale. There might be good reasons for the divergence, and the reasons need to be heard and understood by the product manager in charge. At the end of the discussion, the group should reach a consensus on the most likely scenario of price-volume reactions. Having said that, it is acceptable if difference in opinions persists if there are valid reasons.

As soon as the demand curve illustrated in Fig. 3.6 is created, you will be able to plot the revenue and profit curves (the latter depends on the availability of cost data). See an example in Fig. 3.7.

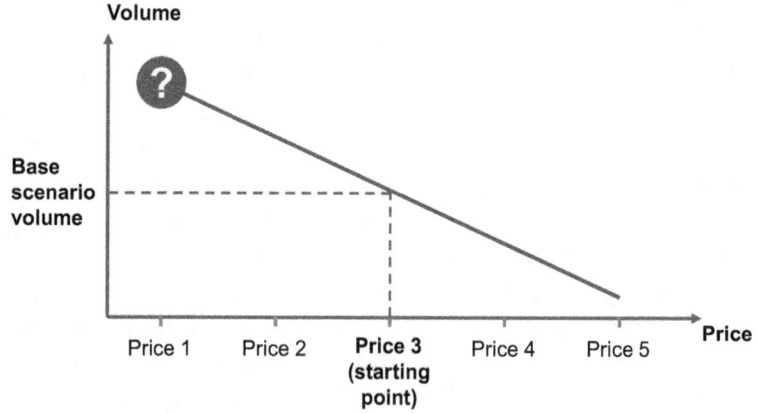

Fig. 3.6 Pricing sandbox exercise

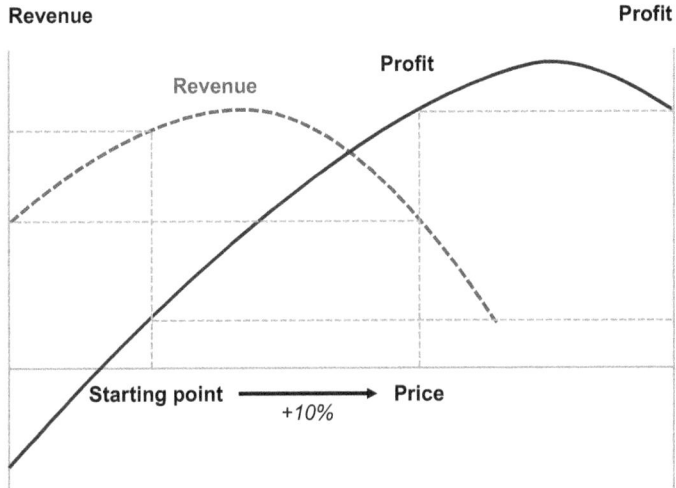

Fig. 3.7 Revenue and profit curve based on pricing sandbox

In this example, there is a trade-off between revenue and profit optimization. A 10% increase in price from the starting point would result in a significant decrease in revenue. Meanwhile, profit growth will outpace revenue decline. Profit would be maximized at a price point where revenue would be further reduced. More revenue or more profit? This question will be addressed in Sect. 3.4.

3.3.2 van Westendorp

van Westendorp Price Sensitivity Meter (PSM) or van Westendorp in short is one of the most widespread market research techniques for identifying the target price range of a new product or service. It is also useful for revealing psychological price thresholds, which play a key role in setting the retail prices. The method was introduced in 1976 by Dutch economist Peter van Westendorp (Wikipedia, 2023i).

To collect data for van Westendorp, you just need to ask four questions as follows.

> **Given [a detailed description of the new product], what price would you consider to be:**

Inexpensive/too cheap?	€_____	(tci)
Acceptable?	€_____	(ai)
Expensive?	€_____	(ei)
Too expensive?	€_____	(tei)

These are open questions so that the respondents can enter whatever numbers they feel like without constraints. However, to make our life easier, we usually

$$tc_i < a_i < e_i < te_i$$

impose the following logic check in the survey:

van Westendorp would work perfectly in a large-scale online survey with thousands of respondents. However, I have also seen it work with a smaller size of under 100. The results have turned out to be plausible just as well.

To gather unbiased high-quality responses, there are a few things that require special attention. First, the description of the new product should be unambiguous and highlight the benefits to potential customers. Try to put yourself in the shoes of the customers and refrain from talking too much about specs and technical details.

Second, the whole purpose of the exercise is to let customers speak freely after being informed of what the new product is supposed to do. Therefore, you should avoid priming the respondents by suggesting, for example, what could make a "*good price range.*" Do not worry about bizarre answers, which will be filtered out or neutralized in the analysis that follows. If you feel compelled to refer to a competitor, it is fine but do make sure to explain both price and value aspects of the competitive product. Then, you are all set. If you enter all responses in a spreadsheet, you will be able to generate a graph such as Fig. 3.8.

The answers to the four abovementioned pricing questions can be translated into a price-volume curve, showing nicely how price acceptance varies across a range that is not preset but is suggested by the respondents. The *Y*-axis % of respondents serves as a proxy for potential sales volume. It is probably easier to understand if you focus on the "*cheap*" curve for the time being.

The intersections of the curves are assigned marketing-jargon-style names which I will spare you here on purpose, because they have little bearing in application. It suffices to know that the area delineated by the intersections indicates a reasonable price range of the new product, based on which you can perform your feasibility analysis to check whether there is a valid business case. It may be clear but still worth mentioning that it is impossible to identify the optimal price with the help of Fig. 3.8 only.

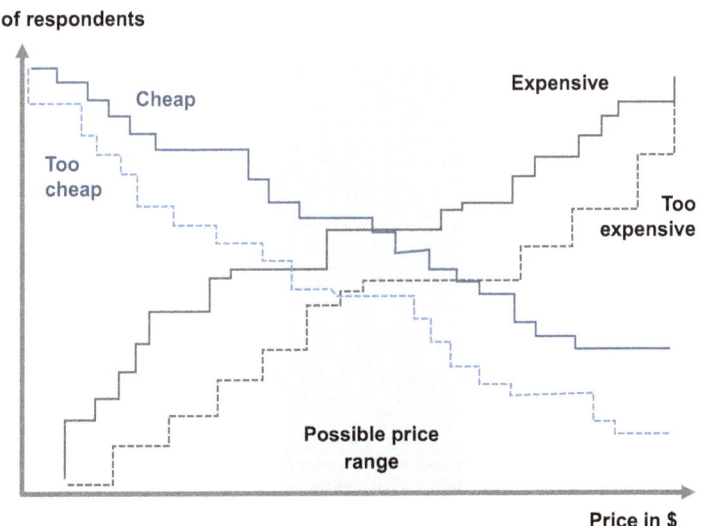

Fig. 3.8 Example of van Westendorp willingness-to-pay curves

There is one potential risk in using the van Westendorp method, which is putting over-proportional spotlight onto price than value so that respondents may understate their true willingness to pay. This problem will be alleviated as the sample size increases and/or respondents can benchmark the new product to an established competitive product that is familiar to them. For the very reason, an increasing number of van Westendorp studies have left out the first question regarding "*what is too cheap a price.*" Logically, product managers and pricing practitioners are much more interested in determining the upper limit than the lower limit of the possible price range, not to mention that the notion of "*too cheap*" may cause confusion or irritation for some respondents.

When we rearrange the dataset, merging all price curves, we can produce a consolidated single price-volume curve, which provides us with additional insights. See an example in Fig. 3.9.

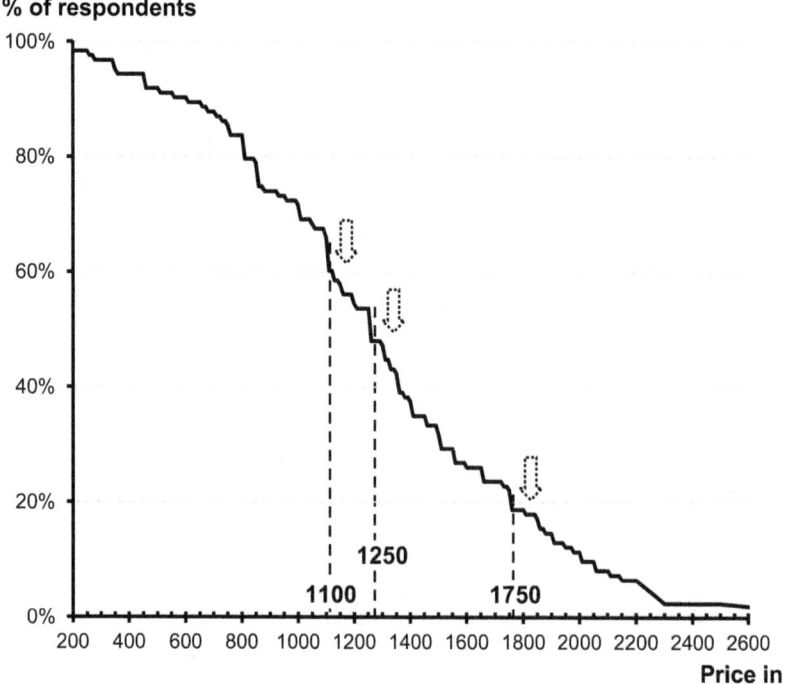

Fig. 3.9 Example of a rearranged van Westendorp price-volume curve

Now we have a price-volume curve in the shape that we are more used to, with price on the X-axis and volume (proxy) on the Y-axis. One significant advantage of the rearrangement of the graph is a visual revelation of the critical price thresholds.

In the example above, price acceptance, an indication of sales volume drops significantly at certain price points such as $1110, $1250, and $1750. It has to do with how the human brain functions. It is theorized that the golden rule in retail pricing is to price the products just under respective price thresholds so that we avoid triggering a significant volume loss. When a retailer prices a product at $99 instead of $100, she/he is buying a lottery ticket. The price is a $1 less earned per head, and the prize is a new customer lured by a two-digit price tag. It takes both math and luck to win the lottery. In Sect. 5.7, you will find a more in-depth examination of pricing endings.

3.3.3 Gabor Granger

There are situations where you are about to introduce an additional product variant following a successful new product launch. From a pricing perspective, the key reference is logically the price of the existing product. The Gabor Granger method, or Gabor Granger in short, is the right pricing technique that you need in this case. This technique was developed in the 1960s by Clive Granger and André Gabor (Wikipedia, 2023c). It is convenient to use Gabor Granger to find the markup or markdown for a new product relative to an existing product.

There are diverse ways to set up a Gabor Granger exercise. The following example shown in Tables 1.1 and 3.1 uses relative price percentages for testing. However, you could also use discrete price points instead.

In this example, variant A is the existing product in the market and serves as our price reference. Variant B is the product for which we want to find an optimal price. The optimum is usually defined as when we achieve the greatest profit from the combination of variants A and B.

For the sake of simplicity, I will use milkshake in this example to illustrate how the Gabor Granger method works. The only difference between the two variants is the size, all else being equal. In practice, you could also

Table 3.1 Example of a Gabor Granger questionnaire

Given [a detailed description of the product differences] and the price difference, which product variant would you choose?

If B costs x% more than A?	A (Basic)	B (Premium)
40%	✓	
30%	✓	
20%		✓
10%		Once B is chosen, the loop ends
5%		

evaluate variants with different features, in case of which the value-added for the customer needs to be laid out clearly.

Milk shake medium size (M) is the existing product variant, whose price is given. We want to know how to price a large size (L) to generate more profit altogether. To assess the willingness to pay for L, we use a price ladder consisting of four steps, corresponding to markups of 40%, 30%, 20%, and 10% relative to M. The test results can be seen in Table 3.2.

As the price gap narrows, the proportion of respondents who favor L over M grows. Only 15% of customers would move to L with a 40% markup; at a 10% markup, as many as 85% of customers would switch. The 20% markup appears to be a price sweet spot. As the retail price of L falls below $5, its popularity grows significantly. The implications of the Gabor Granger exercise are displayed in Table 3.3.

We are mainly concerned with the profit potential of the combination of M + L. It turns out that a 20% markup for L would be optimal from a profit point view. It also checks out in the sanity check, as it is apparently a good deal for the customers—while the content (value) increases by approximately 34%, the sacrifice (price) only goes up by 20%! Not bad, isn't it?

It might have already crossed your mind that Gabor Granger can also be used for new product pricing. We just need to use discrete price points and it should work. This is true. However, I advise caution because unlike

Table 3.2 Results of price test—milk shake

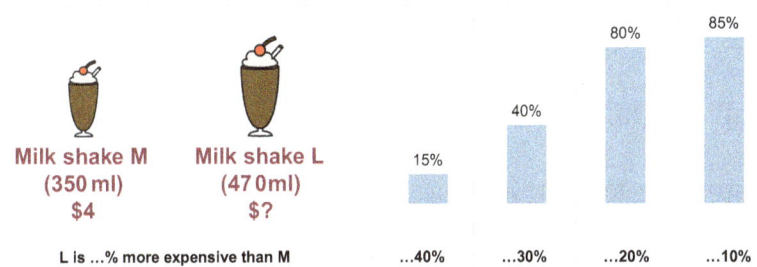

Table 3.3 Financial impact of price test—milk shake

Product variant	Milk shake	M	Milk shake	L
Content in ml	350 ml	470 ml
Retail price	$4	$4.8
Volume split	20%	80%
Profit lift vs. M only	+12%	

van Westendorp, you are burdened with predefining the price points for testing. It can be a tricky task, as you are supposed to know a priori the should-be price range from your customer's perspective. If you miss it, "garbage-in, garbage-out" will be your fate. The safest bet is to make no prior assumptions about willingness to pay.

It is worth noting that, like van Westendorp, Gabor Granger is robust in terms of sample size. In an ideal world, you would apply Gabor Granger in a large-scale online survey. However, it could also function well in a focus group with 10–15 participants. There will always be outliers. Outliers in a large online survey can be filtered out based on the plausibility check of the respondents' responses to other survey questions;

in a focus group, you will have the opportunity to discuss the reasons for any significant divergence, which may lead to the generation of new insights. If the researcher understands the limitations of various methodologies, she or he will be able to make the most of them.

3.3.4 Conjoint Analysis

Conjoint is a magical word that signifies to bring everything together. Conjoint analysis, in contrast to pricing techniques such as van Westendorp and Gabor Granger, is a so-called *indirect* pricing method. Its design is far more complex than that of direct pricing approaches as conjoint does an X-ray of people's minds, decoding the buying choice. We can not only determine the willingness to pay and demand curves using conjoint analysis and the associated simulation model, but we can also find ways to influence customers' preferences by modifying certain product aspects.

Conjoint analysis originated in mathematical psychology and was developed by marketing professor Paul E. Green. Today, it is used in many of the social sciences and applied sciences including marketing, product management, and operations research (Wikipedia, 2023a).

There are various types of conjoint designs. The central premise, however, is the same: it requires trade-offs between features, which can be roughly viewed as value drivers (see Sect. 1.3) that comprise a product's value.

For example, the value of an electric vehicle may be drilled down to the following attributes: brand, electric range, power, equipment, and price. Respondents in a conjoint survey will be asked to choose their most preferred product from different product mockups that consist of the same set of attributes. However, the parameters (levels) of the attributes vary. As an example, the power attribute in a car conjoint design may include parameters such as 700 hp, 800 hp, and 1000 hp.[2]

All attributes and respective parameters must be configured in advance, which might be difficult if the researcher is not familiar enough with the

---

[2] Conjoint designs that allow respondents to specify their product preferences may result in varied attributes as well as parameters being shown.

conceived product and competitive offers. This is the first challenge in carrying out a conjoint analysis. Figure 3.10 shows a trade-off mockup in a conjoint survey.

In a typical conjoint survey, the respondents will be shown a dozen screens like this with different product concepts. The exact number of screens depends on the complexity of the conjoint design. The more attributes and parameters to be evaluated, the more screens that the respondents must click through, all else being equal. This is a second challenge that faces the researcher, i.e., how to keep the complexity at bay. The quality of the responses drops considerably as the survey becomes longer.

The algorithm incorporated in the backend of conjoint software will determine what kind of impact different attribute-parameter combinations may have on the respondents' preference/purchase decision. At the end, each parameter will be assigned a utility value. You can imagine utilities to be the common currency to quantify value (driver), including price, which is also a value driver in a broader sense. Thanks to utilities we can modify existing products or create new products with different

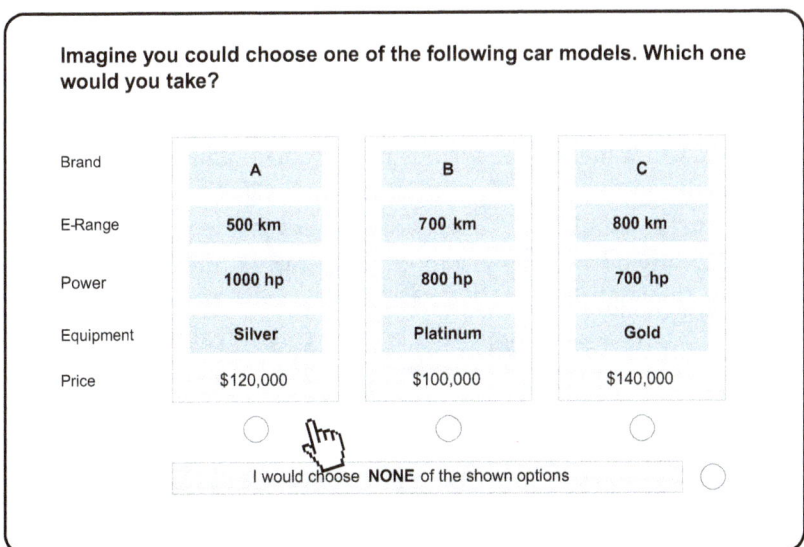

Fig. 3.10 Conjoint trade-off mockup

parameters. The higher the total utilities a product has, the greater the odds the customers would choose it over others. Figure 3.11 shows how utilities for selected features vary, following the electric vehicle conjoint example.

The graphs in Fig. 3.11 show us the utilities for different parameters of three attributes, i.e., electric range, equipment, and price. Because all parameters are denoted in utilities, we can…

(a) …specify the relative importance of each attribute for the purchase decision and
(b) …quantify the monetary value (price) of each parameter on an aggregate level

Be aware that these utility curves mentioned above are only useful on an aggregate level! That is, every potential customer will have her/his unique curves. As a result, when we model preference shares (a surrogate for deserved market shares), we study individual utilities rather than aggregate utilities. The computation and calibration processes are overly complex, posing a third challenge for the researcher.

Using a market simulator based on conjoint data, we will be able to find the optimal price based on our goals, such as revenue, market share, or profit optimization. Unlike other direct pricing methods, we can also tweak the value side of the price-value equation by swapping out a low-utility parameter with a higher one for our new product, which has impact on profit amidst an interplay of revenue and cost variation due to product adaptation. The simulation is a repetitive process that requires both experience and creativity, resulting in a fourth challenge for the researcher.

Despite highlighting all these challenges with conjoint analysis, I remain a huge fan of the approach because it is arguably the only technique that delivers extensive insights into both price and value. As we can see, conjoint analysis as a research tool is effective, but not necessarily efficient, and finally prone to error. It is nearly impossible to execute a conjoint study successfully in-house since it necessitates cross-disciplinary competence in strategy, marketing, market research, pricing, analytics, statistics, psychology, and other fields. It is strongly advised that you seek professional assistance with your conjoint analysis.

3 Let Us Get Started 41

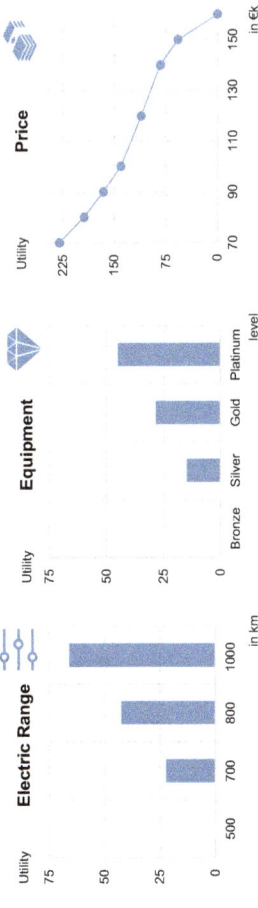

Fig. 3.11 Example of utility curves

3.3.5 Price Experiment

Sometimes product managers conduct price experiments on a small scale before the official product launch—in selected locations, channels, or specific customer groups for a brief period. You may not be aware, but many companies conduct price experiments—from startups to Fortune 500 companies—the size of the business does not play a decisive role here. It makes the most sense when you believe the target price would surpass a critical price threshold, risking a massive loss of sales.

Several price points will be assessed and compared in terms of impact on sales volume during a price experiment, which is similar to a tournament in some ways. The price that brings in the most money will be crowned as the winner.

There are two types of product managers who conduct price experiments. They share the same motivation to reduce uncertainty in pricing. However, the outcome is completely the opposite. Why is that?

The first type of product manager has done all the research and has determined the best price range to pursue. They may have also had specific price points in mind. Price experiments are used to validate their hypothesis and pick the winner.

In contrast, the second type of product managers has barely done any research. Maybe they have looked up the prices of their supposed competitors and done the cost calculation. They are really experimenting without knowing what to expect. Remember I talked about my reservations on using Gabor Granger for new product pricing? Maybe will never be. The same reason applies here too. You should always enter price experiments with sound assumptions; otherwise, you risk testing the wrong price points and arriving at incorrect conclusions; you would be better off without the price experiments.

I have been in contact with the founder and CEO of a techwear [3] startup for a long time. One of its strongest selling points is functional fabrics developed in house. Traditionally, the company specialized in

---

[3] Techwear is a fashion style that combines functionality with style and the appropriate aesthetics. Pockets, lockers, clasps, and straps, as well as other useful accessories are featured in this style of clothing which uses special materials, appropriate design, and properties that ensure breathability, freedom of movement, water resistance, and comfort (Aesthetics Wiki, 2023).

indoor clothing. The CEO had made up his mind to expand into outdoor clothing to capitalize on its expertise in specialty fabrics and fuel future growth. The outdoor clothing market was significantly larger than the indoor clothing market. Meanwhile, the competition was much tougher. Pricing for the new category would be more difficult as well; it was uncharted territory for the company with little experience or brand awareness in the outdoor clothing market. I was convinced of two things after numerous interactions with him.

First, he recognized the significance of pricing or pricing strategy in general; second, he was heavily invested in the new outdoor business. However, he then said something that has perplexed me to this day. In complete confidence, he was providing me with an update on the new product launch:

> I hired a well-known designer who previously worked for Brand X. I have identified 7 to 8 different fabrics that would be suitable for outdoor clothing. I will test them all in our retail stores before settling on one or two to keep complexity and cost under control.
>
> We have also done some pricing research. We would most likely aim for a premium price positioning as in indoor clothing. We plan to evaluate a few price points alongside the fabrics in the coming months.

I nodded approvingly and asked:

"How did you come up with the price points to be tested?"
He: "We compared ourselves to the market leaders and examined our cost structure to ensure profitability."
I: "Did you speak to any potential customers?"
He: "Yes, we interviewed about a dozen customers who were shopping for indoor clothing at our retail stores. Their feedback was overwhelmingly positive."
I: "That's it?"
He: "That's it."

The conversation ended at this point. I was irritated and frustrated for several reasons. First, he was not really conducting a price experiment. Instead, he was conducting a blind test. Directly asking customers about their willingness to pay is rarely a clever idea, as vanity may cause people to exaggerate their willingness to pay.

Second, the core of the customer base for outdoor clothing does not necessarily overlap with the existing customer base. It is too bold an assumption to make.

Third, price experiments are meant for the sprint toward product launch. Customers will never be able to tell you which of the seven or eight fabrics is the best. Furthermore, experimenting with the acceptance of features is extremely costly. It would be much more efficient to narrow the choice set in advance by conducting a focus group or something similar.

Fourth, benchmarking with competitors was only superficial without understanding how customers make decisions and how the new product could differentiate itself from the competition.

Do not misunderstand me. I am totally in favor of price experiments. Because there is so much time and money at stake with a new product launch, one cannot be too cautious. I just do not like the fact that so many product managers believe price experiments are a panacea and a quick fix. No, they are not. They are goalkeepers. There will be nothing to keep if there are no goals.

Crowdfunding platforms are convenient for price experiments. Let us look at an example of a water flosser project on Kickstarter.com. Instafloss is the product in question. It replaces manual flossing with high-speed water flossing, which can reduce accidental damage to gums while achieving a better cleaning effect at the same time.

Water flossing is not a new species and has been around for a while. The main selling point of Instafloss is its high efficiency, as it can finish the job in 10 s. In contrast, the conventional method of manual flossing will take approximately 1 min. Figure 3.12 displays three different options that are available on Kickstarter:

Let us look at the facts first. Both options 1 and 2 are early-bird options, each of which includes one piece of the device. The only difference between these two is the price. The first one is priced at $119, which is $60 cheaper than the estimated retail price, while the second one is priced $10 higher than Option 1. Option 3 is labeled as the best price offer with two devices for $199, with a total saving of $160.

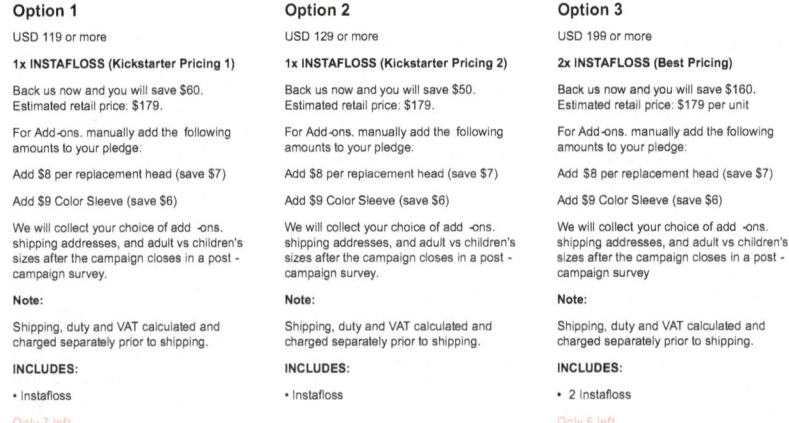

Fig. 3.12 Instafloss pricing options

Although the versioning of options may be inadvertent, there is a price experiment in action. What can we take away from this experiment?

1. **Price levels**. It may not be obvious at first glance. The coexistence of options 1 and 2 is reminiscent of a Gabor Granger reality show. Customers' willingness to pay is indicated by the rate at which each option's inventory depletes.

    Consider the following hypothetical situation: Option 1 sells out in under an hour, and Option 2 ships only two units in 2 weeks. What does it mean? Option 1 is likely to be underpriced, while Option 2 is likely to be overpriced. The best price is most likely between $119 and $129. If Option 2 is also sold out in a fleeting period, I am inclined to introduce a higher priced option to see how it performs.

    A word of caution: the number of units assigned to either option should be the same, otherwise the comparison will be biased.

2. **Product bundling**. The third option is a bundle of two devices. Generally, a bundle consisting of different products is more common—think of value menus in fast-food restaurants. Nevertheless, a bundle of two water flossers could make sense in certain cases. For example, someone is so convinced of the product that she or he would like to buy two units right away for use for the entire family, or to keep

one and gift another to a friend. The bundle offers good value for money (approximately a 45% discount!) for customers who do appreciate the benefit of the bundle. The take rate of the third option alludes to the demand for such bundles. If there was another option for a bundle with a different price point, we could also assess the willingness to pay for the bundles.

A word of caution: if you later find pristine Instafloss at low prices on eBay, they may come from the bundle buyers.

3. **Add-ons** are available for all options at a reduced price: $ 8 for replacement heads and $ 9 for color sleeves. Add-on is a clever way to increase revenue. However, I find it difficult to sell add-ons at the beginning, when customers are not even familiar with the "core" product. Add-ons would be more effective in the presence of a well-established core product that serves as a value reference, as customers would struggle to comprehend the communicated savings otherwise.

A word of caution: if the benefit of the add-ons is evident, providing them at the time of a new product launch may still make sense. If it is true, there is no need for a discount.

All the information presented above dates to 2019, when I first discovered the Instafloss project on Kickstarter. In 2023, while drafting this book, I looked up the official website of Instafloss out of curiosity. The retail price was $199, which was $20 more than the 2019 estimated retail price. There was no bundling available. Sleeves were not listed as an add-on. Replacement heads (now marketed as mouthpieces) cost $19.99. If you select auto-refill every 3 months, the price drops to $12.99. It is up to you to decide whether the price experiment on Kickstarter.com served its purpose.

Price experiments are a popular pricing technique among product managers. However, as the examples above demonstrate, there are numerous pitfalls at the same time. Price experiments, when properly prepared and used, can be an enormously powerful tool for improving your understanding of your customers and making better decisions. They cannot, however, replace all other due pricing work.

3.3.6 Connecting the Dots

After introducing five different methods for determining WTP and demand curves, we still have a few critical questions to address: how do pricing practitioners put all of this into practice? Which techniques should I use? In what kind of order? What if the outcomes from various sources differ?

In practice, there are several ways to arrive at a pricing decision. While I understand the need for a tailored solution, one principle should always be followed: the *coarse-to-fine* principle. In other words, you should have an idea of the following questions from the start.

Who is the target customer?
What is the product good for?
What is my competitive edge/USP?
What would be a reasonable price range?
…

The answers to these questions will become clearer, after you have completed adequate research, analysis, and evaluation. Depending on how certain you are about the answers to these questions, you may be able to skip a few steps in the general pricing route as illustrated in Fig. 3.13.

The general pricing route consists of a total of nine steps. The first four steps unfold internally, with an emphasis on ideation. By the end of Step 4, you should have reached an agreement on a rough equation of the product's value and price from potential customers' point of view.

Steps 5 through 8 set out a range of activities toward external validation, from coarse to fine, from qualitative to quantitative. Finally, in Step 9, you will bring everything together and decide what to sell, how much to charge, and how to charge it.

Fig. 3.13 General pricing route

The key actions at each step are briefly described below:

1. **Explorative research:** you notice an unmet customer need or have a cool technology (prototype) in mind. You want to collect ideas and benchmarks to see what is already and what might be there for you.
2. **Ideation:** you develop ideas on potential product concepts including main selling points with reference to specific customer use cases. Ideally, you should also have your estimate on willingness to pay of the target customers to guide further development of the product idea.
3. **Internal interviews:** you consult with experts primarily internally to assess ideas for technical and commercial feasibility. You may also want to seek expert advice outside your own organization at times. You should have an idea of the product-market-price fit at the end of this step. Section 3.3.1 can be useful in this step.
4. **Internal survey:** this step makes sense if there is a large group of people who could help bring the new idea to fruition. It is especially valuable when you require input from multiple geographies or markets. Section 3.3.2 or 3.3.3 will come in handy. By the end of this step, the product prototype should have emerged.
5. **Pilot customer interviews:** it is time to listen to the voice of the customer. The main purpose is to observe how target customers react to the new product in the context of their respective use cases. This is the time to eliminate any blind spots or misperceptions.
6. **Focus groups:** you present images or ideally product prototypes to a small group of people and hold in-depth discussions about key aspects of the new product in comparison with competitors' products. Depending on the sample size, you may also want to make use of Sect. 3.3.2 or 3.3.3.
7. **Creative meeting:** you present a revised product concept to a small group of experts who may be KOLs,[4] heavy users or industry veterans, based on output from Step 6. You are getting close to finalizing the product concept. The goal of the creative meeting is to make final adjustments before conducting large-scale testing.

---

[4] KOLs: key opinion leaders

8. **Large-scale customer survey:** thus far, all assumptions have been made/assessed using small samples. To obtain a better sense of how the new product would fare in the real world, it is highly recommended to conduct a large-scale customer survey, which includes at least 300 effective respondents[5] in a specific market (mainly applicable to the B2C sector. The sample size and survey format for the B2B sector will differ). All pricing methods from Sect. 3.3.1 through 3.3.6 are applicable in the survey. However, you must be aware of the trade-off here. The longer the questionnaire, the less robust the results.
9. **Simulation & Decision:** it is a critical last step that is often unfortunately skipped. Thus far, you have collected a lot of data. Numbers need to be synthesized and analyzed to inform the final decision to find the price. By now, we have productized the price/willingness to pay. It is time to strategize the price, as decisions must be made on which goals the pricing strategy is supposed to achieve.

It is worth noting that the new product development may end at any step of the pricing route, should the cost (value to offer) outweigh the benefit (price to charge). To see how it works, imagine two extreme scenarios as follows:

Scenario A: you are convinced that you are clear about almost everything including target customers, use cases, USP, and so on. The target price is the only missing puzzle piece.

Scenario B: you believe the new product has exciting potential, but you are unsure about the rest.

If you find yourself in a situation like Scenario A, consider yourself fortunate. If you know you have something unique and valuable to offer, you will have a better chance at pricing.

The gravity of the pricing work leans toward validating the value perception and the should-be price. Beware! If the new product is disruptively innovative, you may be on the verge of creating a new market for

---

[5] Effective respondents are potential consumers who take the survey seriously and do not rush through the questions.

which no established demand curve exists. The fate of the new product is determined by how you define the target customers and the corresponding use cases—the willingness to pay of the target customers plays a vital role in determining the potential of the new market.

Under these conditions, you will most likely begin somewhere between Steps 6 and 8, with the main task being to challenge or confirm the product concept and corresponding willingness to pay.

If you find yourself in Scenario B, you should probably try to go through the entire pricing route described in Fig. 3.13. It is critical, in my opinion, to keep the value-price equation in mind throughout the journey. When the targeted price falls out of love with the perceived value, you must have the fortitude to call it quits before it is too late.

3.4 Price It!: The Moment of Truth (MoT)

You have worked hard so far, studying the market, developing the product, and weighing your strategic options; now it is time to go for the goal, the moment of truth. It is a tough time because there will always be things in the market that you cannot predict. Even the most sophisticated simulation model in the world cannot solve all your problems.

At this point, the best advice I could give to any product manager is as follows:

Listen to and act on facts.

If the product is mundane, the price should be low (if you still want to launch it); if it is unique, the price should be high. Taking the middle ground is not a safe bet. Instead, it is a sign of weakness, indicating that you are unsure about what you are selling and what your customers are buying.

In fact, playing it safe is more common with high-value products. The founder of a high-tech startup revealed his pricing strategy for the company's next big thing:

When compared to competitors, our new product seems to be unrivaled in every way. We plan to price the new product close to the price level of the market leader so that we can overtake them.

There is a logical fallacy. If the new product is a knockout, it will attract customers at a higher price than the competition. The iPhone is a classic example in this regard, commanding global market leadership despite its high price. Another good example is Dyson, which invented and owns the cordless vacuum cleaner category, where competitors' products would sell for a fraction of the price of Dyson's (Yang, 2020). If the opposite is true—the new product is lackluster, then playing it safe would imply a significant markdown from original price—putting a strain on its financial feasibility.

Self-imposed low pricing strategy despite strong value proposition makes sense only when there is significant economy of scale to profit from. Costco's two-part pricing scheme is an example of how this could work. Basically, what Costco does is to provide its members with low-cost products while making most of its profit from membership sales rather than product sales. Costco's low-priced business model can only be sustained because of its enormous bargaining power with suppliers due to large purchase volumes.

3.5 Summary

- There is only one definition of business purpose: to create a customer.
- Businesses must turn a profit to live up to their purpose. Value creation must be rewarded to finance innovations on a sustainable basis.
- Product-market-fit is nice to have. Only a product-market-price fit will result in a viable business case.
- The value creation journey begins and ends with the customer, whose willingness-to-pay determines the destiny of the journey.
- A unique selling point (USP) does not hold unless customers are willing to pay for it.
- The KANO model (Figs. 3.3, 3.4 and 3.5) assists product managers with product design and USP creation.

- There are a variety of pricing techniques to reveal customers' willingness to pay.

    - The pricing sandbox (Figs. 3.6 and 3.7)
    - van Westendorp (Figs. 3.8 and 3.9)
    - Gabor Granger (Tables 3.1, 3.2 and 3.3)
    - Conjoint analysis (Figs. 3.10 and 3.11)
    - Price experiment (Fig. 3.12)

- There are different routes to reach a pricing decision, while one principle should always apply, i.e., the coarse-to-fine principle. The nine-step general pricing route (Fig. 3.13) will guide you through the process of new product pricing.
- Even the most sophisticated simulation model in the world cannot solve all your problems.
- If the product is mundane, the price should be low (if you still want to launch it); if it is unique, the price should be high.
- Self-imposed low pricing strategy despite strong value proposition makes sense only when there is significant economy of scale to profit from.

4

Keep the Ball Rolling

How do you adjust pricing if you have made it past the startup stage and the business keeps expanding? To begin, you should dig deeper into your customer profiles.

Consider the following anonymized example of a SaaS[1] company. After years of struggle, the company has finally established itself in the market, slipping into a comfortable zone. It has been sticking to its original pricing gig with only minor cosmetic changes—a phenomenon I call pricing inertia. Nobody cares about how to improve pricing if the business is doing well.

Its pricing plan consists of three tiers: *Entry*, *Advanced*, and *Pro*, whose monthly prices are $19, $39, and $59, respectively. Different features are packaged into different tiers. In terms of the take rates, 40% of the customers land in the entry option, 25% choose *Advanced*, and remaining 35% opt for *Pro*. It yields a monthly ARPU[2] of $38.

The fact that the largest chunk of customers settle for the lowest pricing tier is unsatisfactory. A bell-shaped distribution of customers across tiers would be more reasonable because the majority of the customers

---

[1] SaaS: software as a service
[2] ARPU: average revenue per user

should find themselves well served in the middle option (the golden middle). The overproportion of the entry option suggests that it may be overpackaged with advanced features, leaving customers with little incentive to upgrade to a higher tier.

A thorough examination reveals that customers' needs and willingness to pay are misaligned, implying that the current packaging and pricing architecture is suboptimal in the sense that some customers overpay for features that they do not require, while others underpay due to a lack of desired features. What if we change the packaging and the pricing? Table 4.1 shows the impact of the makeover.

We are able to reshuffle the features across the tiers and add a new tier at the top with some new features without incurring any additional costs for the company. Everything else remains the same. As a result, ARPU would rise by 7%, with the added benefit of gaining more potential customers due to more appealing packaging and pricing architecture. It is worth noting that the 7% increase in revenue will be fully captured on the bottom line because the cost has not changed. If the company has a net profit margin of 20%, the suggested price retouching would result in a 35% increase in net profit. Not bad, right? How can we do it systematically? We should begin by taking stock of the current customer base.

Table 4.1 Repricing of a SaaS product

Options	Current		New	
	Price	Customers	Price	Customers
- Entry	$19	40	$19	25
- Advanced	$39	25	$29	35
- Pro	$59	35	$49	25
- Platinum			$89	15

	Current	New	%Difference
ARPU	$38	$41	7%

4.1 Understand Your Customers

Every successful business started out with the mission to fulfill the needs of a particular customer group. The initial product and pricing architecture is laid out for that purpose, which needs regular maintenance, and this is why:

With the passage of time, early adopters may develop new demands that could not have been anticipated at the outset; newcomers may place greater value on features that were developed on the side. It is a common occurrence because the only constant in our era is change.

Regular updates of customer profiles shed light on these changes and are beneficial for achieving better results, as they could reduce customer churn which usually originates from dissatisfactory products or poor shopping experiences. Studies show that the cost of acquiring new customers is five times higher than the cost of retaining existing customers. While acquisition allows you to increase the number of customers you have, customer retention allows you to maximize the value of customers you have already captured (Optimove, 2023).

Under the umbrella of customer profiling there are four common variants (Evans, 2021):

1. **Demographic profiling**. It is probably the most well-known type of customer profiling among all. It describes customers in terms of age, gender, income, marital status, education level, and so on.
2. **Geographic profiling**. It is self-explaining and straightforward. However, it is also useless unless one can find ways to treat regional groups effectively.
3. **Psychographic profiling**. It investigates target audience's habits, hobbies, interests, and life goals. It goes deeper into how the customer's mind functions, which is helpful for finding out what might resonate with the target audience most effectively.
4. **Behavioral profiling**. Understanding your customers' behavior throughout their buyer journeys (for example, following an AIDA

model[3]) is crucial to providing them with what they truly need. Focus of behavioral profiling lies in identifying customers' purchasing and engagement/usage patterns.

These variants are not mutually exclusive, while the first one is probably what most people envision when they think of customer profiling. Companies are increasingly commission studies that cover all aspects of customer profiling to be thorough. The way how the survey data is interpreted becomes decisive for the quality of customer profiling.

The traditional approach to survey data analysis assumes that customers' personal profiles (primarily Variant 1, and to a lesser extent Variant 2) and life attitudes (primarily Variant 3) are predictive of their preferences and shopping behavior (primarily Variant 4), which is often not given enough weight in segmentation. This assumption, however, is questionable because the claim of a correlation between what customers look like (or how they perceive their lives) and how they shop is, at best, speculative. As a result, the validity of traditional customer segmentation is called into question. The segments are jumbled because the similarities are too great to ignore, and the differences are too minor to affect. Customer profiling too often turns out to be a marketing ploy decorated with fancy names (for example, names like *Open-minded Souls* or *Thoughtful Value Seekers* would tell you nothing but nothing) for all superficially created segments that do not result in actionable measures in the end. After all, a married 60-year-old man in the city and a divorced 30-year-old woman in the countryside can both feel the same way about a product and use it in the same way.[4]

To act on customer profiling, we must first determine whether there are distinct use cases, because use cases reveal information about customers' value perception and, as a result, their willingness to pay. This is what matters in the end. A use case can be characterized by three aspects, each of which can lead to concrete actions to be taken:

---

[3] The AIDA model, tracing the customer journey through Awareness, Interest, Desire, and Action, is perhaps the best-known marketing model amongst all the classic marketing models (Hanlon, 2023).

[4] Product examples may include dairy products, beverages, stream movies, hotel accommodations, and so on.

1. **The core**: what features about the product do customers like or dislike?
    Actions: product optimization, versioning adjustment
2. **The rationale**: what problems does the customer want to solve?
    Actions: value communication, pricing adjustment
3. **The journey**: how do customers inform themselves about the product? Where do they shop? Who else would influence their purchase decisions?
Actions: marketing budget optimization, sales optimization

How can use-case-based profiling be put into practice? The easiest way is to conduct regular customer surveys to keep updated on the pulse of the customers. The survey questionnaire does not need to be complicated as long as it addresses the key questions mentioned above. Face-to-face interviews or focus groups that allow for in-depth discussions are recommendable every now and then.

4.2 Expand, Differentiate and Price Smartly

In the initial stages of a company, the product manager should prioritize developing a minimum viable product, or an MVP that resonates with early adopters, as soon as possible. The same principle should apply to pricing—MVP, in this context, should also refer to a minimum viable price, which is typically a simple price point with no strings attached at the start.

Pricing must evolve over time as the product becomes more sophisticated to meet the diverse needs of customers. A uniform price will no longer suffice. It is time to think about price differentiation.

As the SaaS example in the beginning of this chapter shows, price differentiation/repricing could boost revenue and profit in a heartbeat. The newly added option *Platinum* would be the largest contributor to the success, as it accounts for 33%[5] of the new ARPU.

---

[5] Total ARPU = $41 in the hypothetical scenario, Platinum ARPU = $13, with the highest revenue share of all options. It is also worth noting that Platinum and Pro would account for 63% of the new ARPU, while Pro accounts for 45% of the old ARPU, representing an 18-percentage point increase in ARPU share attributed to high-end options.

Figure 4.1 illustrates the power of price differentiation, where two schemes of pricing are shown for comparison, with uniform price as a starting point on the left-hand side and differentiated price as a contrast on the right. For the sake of simplicity, let us assume that there is no operating cost (remember it, as this is an important assumption here). The shaded areas represent the revenue and profit under either of the pricing schemes.

On the one hand, the uniform price is easy to implement, which results in a profit rectangular. Obviously, the price-demand curve is inadequately exploited, as a sizable area remains unexploited for a lack of suitable offers.

On the other hand, the differentiated price is somewhat complex to set up. However, it pays off financially, with more space under the price-demand curve being occupied, as the profit rectangular transforms itself into a triangle. In an ideal scenario, you would be able to double the profit with the change to differentiated price.

We should distinguish between price discrimination and price differentiation. The former is illegal in most legislations around the world, as customers are unfairly treated, paying different prices for the same product or service. Price differentiation, however, is well accepted in most situations, provided that the seller can justify the price differences with differences in offerings. Life examples of price differentiations around us are abundant. Let us look at three examples of various natures.

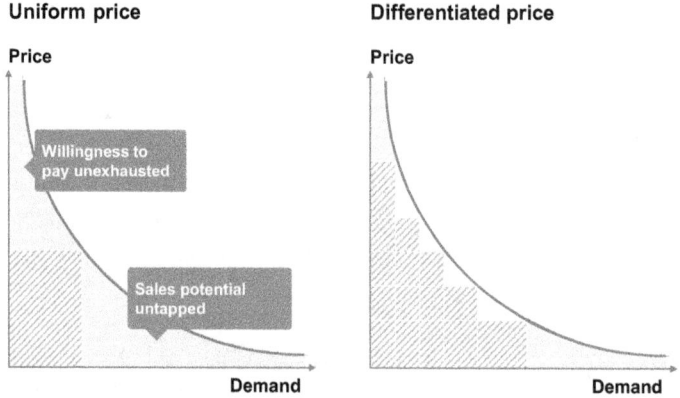

Fig. 4.1 From uniform price to differentiated price

1. **Product**

    Carmakers are good at packaging their products. They are experts at offering various trim lines or packages to exploit customers' willingness to pay. There are feature packages tailored to luxury or performance-oriented drivers, as well as a plethora of add-ons available. Established OEMs in the combustion era are used to approaching packaging in this manner.

    In contrast, the electric vehicle newcomers tend to have a much slimmer product architecture, a trend set by Tesla. Interestingly, the newcomers have gradually enriched their offers in recent years, moving away from monotonic standardization toward prismatic differentiation.

    Rationale for price differentiation: customers have different preferences for how their cars should be equipped.

2. **Service**

    The travel industry has been a forerunner in price differentiation. Almost all full-service airlines offer seats on the plane at least in three different classes: economy, business, and first class. To capitalize on differentiation opportunities, many airlines would even add a mezzanine class between economy class and business class.

    Fun fact: there is no universal definition of what constitutes the mezzanine class, and airlines are free to be creative with their naming. The most well-known among all is likely Premium Economy. However, you may also hear terms like Premium Plus or Economy Plus. Pricing logic for the mezzanine class would vary significantly across airlines.

    Rationale for price differentiation: travelers' budgets for the same route would differ, most notably between business and leisure travelers.

3. **Retail**

Many large grocery stores carry their own brands in addition to well-known brand names. These brands are also known as white labels or private labels. Backed up by the retailer's reputation, private labels are popular for their value for money—comparable quality as national brands—however, priced at a significant discount. They are an important source of revenue and profit for the retailers.

Some retailers use the namesake for their private labels, such as Aldi and REWE; others create new brand names that appear unrelated to their origins. One of the most well-known examples is Kirkland Signature, which accounts for approximately a quarter of Costco's total revenue (Nesbit, 2023). It has become such a strong brand in its own right that many customers would come to Costco because of Kirkland Signature. *Rationale for price differentiation*: some consumers place less emphasis on brand and more emphasis on product functionality than others.

Price differentiation manifests itself in different price levels in the examples above. A car with a better trim line would cost $5000 more; business class on a flight from Shanghai to Frankfurt costs four times that of economy class; and a Kirkland Signature cookware set is 20% less expensive than a well-known German brand. Is that all?

No, price differentiation does not end at the price level. The price level refers to how much you will charge. It is only one perspective on price differentiation. Another perspective is to reconsider the pricing metric, which is related to how to charge. See an example below.

Michelin developed a new tire that has the potential to last 25% longer than the previous model. However, it is nearly impossible to price the new product 25% higher than the old one because the customers, who are mostly fleets, are extremely price-sensitive or have tight budgets. As a result, adoption of the new product faces significant challenges. The solution is to switch from a one-time transactional pricing model to a pay-per-use pricing model, which better aligns the value that customers receive with the price that they must pay. Customers pay by the mile for the use of a tire, and if the tires last 25% longer as claimed by Michelin, they will be rewarded with a 25% price premium.

It is not a zero-sum game, as the customers also benefit: they will only be charged for the tires when the trucks are on the road rolling. It is also advantageous from a business planning and controlling point of view (Simon, 2015).

Despite all benefits, price differentiation bears a risk, namely, price contamination. Price contamination occurs when a high willingness-to-pay customer trades down to a lower priced product. The customer may suffer because of the lower priced product providing less value; the customer may not suffer because of being overserved and overcharged initially. Profit leakage emerges either way, which is unwelcome news for the business. We need to fix it.

4.3 Build Fences Early on

In marketing jargon, the mechanism used to prevent price contamination is referred to as fencing. As illustrated in Fig. 4.2, the goal of fencing is to create barriers that encourage customers to stay in a higher-end option while discouraging them from moving down to a lower-end option, or both.

As the word *fence* implies, it is practically almost impossible to build Chinese Walls between price options. Smart shoppers always find their way to get around the fences. Fencing is built with tolerance of exceptions. Nevertheless, product managers should take efforts to mend the fences and develop new tricks over time. The fences can be good, bad, and sometimes even ugly from a customer's perspective.

4.3.1 The Good

A good fence relies on customers' self-selection with little intervention required from the seller, making it the most customer-friendly type of fence possible. Customers are at ease across the fences because they are well served where they are. The seller does not need to do anything special to shepherd the buyers in this ideal situation.

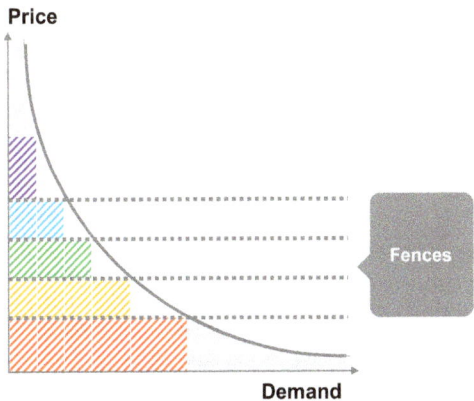

Fig. 4.2 Price fencing

It looks simple for the seller, as the good fence appears to be unnecessary. The truth is that in order to be good, the seller must put in a lot more effort upfront in perfecting the offer design. The KANO model, which we described in Sect. 3.2 in the context of discovering a unique selling point, is one way to go about it.

To recap, the KANO model divides a product's features into five categories: must-have, expected, excitement, indifferent, and killers. The seller tends to serve rather homogeneous customers (in this case also known as early adopters) at the start of a venture, by choice, with survival being the primary goal. As time passes, preferences naturally diverge into different camps, with new or reinvented use cases. As a result, a universal KANO model that fits all will no longer be appropriate. Averaging differences is both convenient and deceptive.

It becomes clear that product managers can no longer work with only one KANO model that entails all customer preferences. Instead, there should be one KANO model per segment. In effect, it means that each segment will have their own must-have, expected, excitement features, and so on. If we can map out all that and design the options accordingly, there is no need for fencing.

4.3.2 The Bad

Fences are bad for customers when it takes time and effort to get around. They incur opportunity costs for customers. The equation of cost–benefit analysis may vary individually. Customers for whom the costs of de-fencing outweigh the benefits will stay put despite appreciating the view across the fence.

Fast-food restaurants use coupons to differentiate and fence customers based on their price sensitivity. In the old days, coupons used to be paper-based. Consumers could use these coupons to buy featured products at a discounted price. Nowadays, coupons are mostly digitalized thanks to the broad adoption of smartphones. The working principle remains the same, although the format now looks different.

E-coupons are available at the fingertips of virtually everyone who uses a smartphone. The hassle of searching and collecting paper-based coupons has long gone. Digitalization has democratized coupons to the benefit of consumers. However, why do McDonald's and Co. continue to bother offering coupons? Because coupons work in lieu of identification cards that reveal the price sensitivity of consumers. Some patrons go to fast-food restaurants because of the shortened waiting time, while others do so because of the low price. The former would attach less importance to the price they pay, being conscious of what they are going to obtain for the price; the latter are constantly on the lookout for deals and promotions. The former tend to be loyal customers; the latter are probably bargain seekers. The former will go to the restaurant without looking for coupons in advance; the latter will check the availability of coupons before entering the door of the restaurant, being it paper-based or digital.

Coupons are bad for some customers because they think of using coupons as an extra hassle that is harmful to their shopping experience. Meanwhile, coupons can be good for others who are happy to trade non-monetary efforts for monetary benefits. For the restaurant operator, the use of coupons pays off if it brings in incremental traffic into the restaurant. The impulsive purchase of the price-sensitive customers may contribute additional revenue and profit.

4.3.3 The Ugly

Things get ugly when it hurts the customer to cross the fence, as the seller takes extreme measures to make customers stay clear of the fence. The following anecdote exemplifies such a case.

The French engineer Jules Dupuit noted the necessity of ugly fencing as early as in 1849. At that time, the third-class wagons on the train did not have a roof. "It is not because of the few thousand Francs which would have to be spent to put a roof over the third class-seats," Dupuit explained. "What the company is trying to do is to prevent the passenger who can pay the second class-fare from traveling third class; it hits the poor, not because it wants to hurt them, but to frighten the rich" (Dupuit, 1849). Let us look at another example.

Once upon a time, it was a widespread practice for telecom operators to bind customers in a high-value package with an extended contract duration from 12 to 24 months. The customers could not downgrade, even if their communications needs had changed during the contract period. Instead, they had to wait out the contract before switching. On the other hand, there was usually no such constraint if a customer wanted to upgrade to a higher-value package. The fence worked like a one-way valve in this case. The trick does its job in the short run. However, it will hurt the telecom operator eventually.

As a disgruntled customer is finally free to switch after the expiration of the current contract, she/he would likely not switch to a lower tariff but switch to another service provider. Down the road, the competition in the telecom market has become so fierce that a new widespread practice emerged to break down each other's fences: telecom service providers carry over not only new customers' existing phone numbers but also the residual value of their current contracts with the incumbent service provider, rendering the time lock meaningless. In fact, all ugly fences do not hold long, as they eventually ruin the relationships between the buyer and the seller.

4.3.4 The Unsaid

Every gun makes its own tune. As you can imagine, the three fences mentioned above are not mutually exclusive. In fact, they may be put in use simultaneously as a multilayer bulwark.

Now let us turn our attention to the Unsaid beyond the Good, the Bad and the Ugly. Thus far, we have elaborated on the defensive nature of fencing, whose main purpose is to prevent trading down. However, fencing also opens doors for luring customers to trade up.

The following is a true story. I met with a coworker in Shanghai where she was spending her vacation. As we chatted, I asked how her trip from Frankfurt to Shanghai was. It turned out that she got lucky and was bumped up to the business class for free.

The nice gesture of the airline paid off, as she decided to get an upgrade for the return flight at her own expense. Therefore, you see, the good fences dividing economy, business and first classes can become even better, when customers coming from the lower tier revisit their cost–benefit equation and adjust the benefit factor upwards.

It is worth noting that the incremental profit decreases as the degree of price differentiation increases. Fencing is not free for the seller. This implies that there must be a level of price differentiation that is optimal. Not only the buyer, but also the seller should constantly perform a cost–benefit analysis on how to go about fencing.

4.4 Meet Price Elasticity

Thus far, I have curbed my enthusiasm not to talk about this single most important concept in price management earlier. Part of the reason is that price elasticity is such a tricky topic that we had better address it after we have covered the pricing basics to avoid misunderstanding. In what follows, I will address four aspects of price elasticity to provide the readers with a holistic view, with the goal of being more pragmatic than theoretical.

4.4.1 The Concept

In layman's terms, price elasticity tells us by how many percentage points more products will be sold (either through more buying customers, or when more products are sold per customer, or both), if the seller reduces the price by a percentage point, or vice versa. Formally, the price elasticity for infinitesimal changes is defined mathematically as in Eq. (4.1):

$$\varepsilon = \frac{\partial q}{\partial p} \times \frac{p}{q} \qquad (4.1)$$

Equation 4.1: Price elasticity

where $\partial q/\partial p$ is the first derivative of the price-response function $q = q(p)$, q is the volume, and p is the price (Yang, 2020).

4.4.2 The Relevance

We discussed the significance of revealing the true willingness to pay, which serves as the factual foundation for pricing. Knowing your customers' willingness to pay will put you at advantage. The most appealing aspect of price elasticity is that it is a trump card. If you know your price elasticity, you can determine the price that results in the highest profit, or whatever financial goal you pursue. Let us walk through the formulas (Barkley, 2023). Prewarning: this may get a bit math-heavy, as much as needed.

There is a useful relationship between marginal revenue (MR) and the price elasticity of demand (E_d). It is derived by taking the first derivative of the total revenue (TR) function. The product rule from calculus is used. The product rule states that the derivative of an equation with two functions is equal to the derivative of the first function times the second, plus the derivative of the second function times the first function, as shown in Eq. (4.2):

$$\frac{\partial(yz)}{\partial x} = \left(\frac{\partial y}{\partial x}\right)z + \left(\frac{\partial z}{\partial x}\right)y \qquad (4.2)$$

Equation 4.2: The product rule

The product rule is used to find the derivative of the total revenue (TR) function. Price can be treated as a function of quantity for a company with market power. Recall that $MR = \frac{\partial TR}{\partial Q}$, and the equation for the elasticity of demand in Eq. (4.1). We can derive the following:

Given TR = $P(Q)Q$, then

$$\frac{\partial TR}{\partial Q} = \left(\frac{\partial P}{\partial Q}\right)Q + \left(\frac{\partial Q}{\partial Q}\right)P$$

$$MR = \left(\frac{\partial P}{\partial Q}\right)Q + P$$

Next, we divide and multiply both sides of the equation by P:

$$\text{MR} = \left[\frac{\left(\frac{\partial P}{\partial Q}\right) Q}{P} \right] P + P = \left[\frac{1}{\text{Ed}}\right] P + P = P\left(1 + \frac{1}{\text{Ed}}\right) = P + \frac{P}{\text{Ed}}$$

Profit maximization is reached when MR = MC, therefore:

$$\text{MC} = \text{MR} = P + \frac{P}{\text{Ed}}$$

We arrange the equation and arrive at Eq. (4.3):

$$\frac{P - \text{MC}}{P} = \text{Profit margin} = -\frac{1}{\text{Ed}} \qquad (4.3)$$

Equation 4.3: The magic formula

It is a magnificent equation. If price elasticity and marginal cost are known, you can calculate the optimal price for profit optimization, presuming that the product in question provides customers with some unique value. It will be a different case, if the product is a commodity and the provider is merely a price taker.

4.4.3 The Limitation

In my view, the most difficult challenge confronted with the magic formula as in Eq. (4.3) is that price elasticity is not something solid written in stone. Instead, price elasticity is fluid, like water.

To illustrate this point, let us look at the three different demand curves (Yang, 2020) in Fig. 4.3.

You will probably recognize demand curve No. 1 from your economics class at the college. It is a classic demand curve in which price and volume

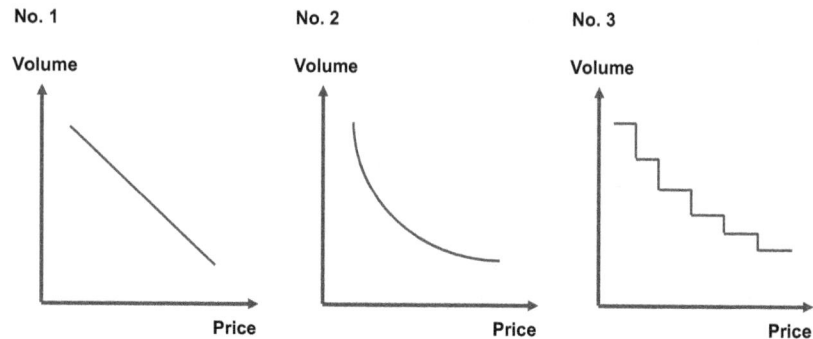

Fig. 4.3 Three different types of demand curves

are perfectly linearly correlated. Does it sound simple? Yes, but there is a catch: linear correlation does not imply constant price elasticity. In fact, price elasticity increases as the price increases along the curve.

Demand flattens out toward the higher end of the price axis in demand curve No. 2, while it is extremely responsive to price changes in the low-price segment. One possible explanation for this phenomenon is that affluent customers in the high-price segment are generally insensitive to price, whereas customers with limited resources in the low-price segment would adeptly adjust their purchase behavior to the price level. Price elasticity is found to be constant along the entirety of demand curve No. 2.

Stepwise demand curve No. 3 is probably more reflective of reality in most cases. It basically says that the relation between price and volume is not a linear continuum. Instead, it will be better described by a series of distinct segments. The demand stays flat within a certain price segment, wherein the price changes would do little to the demand. However, once the price falls at either end of a segment on the curve, the demand will change abruptly. In other words, price elasticities equal zero within the range of respective price segments, in which customers base their purchase decisions on value drivers other than price.

In demand curve No. 3, it is crucial for product managers and pricing practitioners to recognize the price segments and the corresponding price thresholds. It has special implications for price promotions, which need to hit a lower price segment to be effective, i.e., to trigger incremental sales volume. If it fails to do so, it will be just giving money away for nothing, since price elasticity will be zero. We go over promotions in greater detail in Chap. 5.

The three demand curves described above are representative of the price elasticity universe; however, they are by no means exhaustive of what is out there. Price elasticity is particularly important input for any price decision. When considering price elasticity, we need to take extra caution because it is fluid instead of static. Experience from the past may or may not apply to the price decision that you must make now.

4.4.4 The Application

To apply price elasticity, we need to obtain price elasticity first. Many product managers and pricing practitioners would dream of having a price elasticity databank. I would love that too. It would make our life so much easier. However, there is none and will be none. The truth is that others' price elasticities will not help you. You must curate your own price elasticity knowledge over time.

Historical data is a main source for obtaining price elasticities. Consider the following example: in the beginning, both price and volume are equal to 100. In the previous period, we registered four price changes. Figure 4.4 depicts the resulting volumes and price elasticities.

The first thing we notice is that volume does not change at all when the price goes up by 5%, which is good for business. Customers begin to react when price changes exceed 10%. Volume decreases at price points 110, 120, and 130, indicating price elasticities of –0.5, –1.0, and –0.8, respectively.[6] On the right side of Fig. 4.4, you can see the corresponding demand curve. So, what have we learned from previous sales data?

1. A 5% price increase is a safe bet, as customers swallow it instead of walking away.
2. We will see some reactions once the price moves up by 10% or more.
3. Price elasticities seem to be moderate in the shown price change range from 5 to 30%, suggesting that the product is rather competitive.

---

[6] The price elasticities shown here are point price elasticities, with fixed at the original price and the volume level indexed to 100.

Price	Volume	Price elasticity
100	100	–
105	100	0
110	95	-0.5
120	80	-1.0
130	75	-0.8

Fig. 4.4 Price elasticity from historical data

If we plug in cost data and calculate revenue and profit for the price scenarios mentioned above, we will generate more insights, as shown in Table 4.2.

Given the underlying price elasticities, revenue is maximized at the price of 105 while profit is maximized at 130. Although we did not record price increases beyond 30%, the odds are that a significant price increase beyond 30% would lead to a massive loss in sales volume. If our goal is to maximize profit, 130 should be fairly close to the ideal price.

You can reconstruct the analysis relatively easily, if you have kept track of price changes in the past and you have a good understanding of volume and cost. This type of analysis suits well with high-turnover products.

However, there is a problem with longtail products. It is common in spare parts businesses that one SKU[7] would be shipped only a few times in a year. To put it in perspective, a sophisticated machinery manufacturer or an MRO[8] distributor may carry millions of such SKUs. In extreme cases, some slow-moving articles may not be sold in a matter of years. As a result of data scarcity, conducting any historical price elasticity analysis would be challenging. A possible workaround solution is to combine homogeneous longtail products to form a homogeneous product group (commonly known as HPG) for data analysis. We can assume that products with certain characteristics will fall into the same price elasticity bucket.

There is one caveat with any historical data analysis: we have been implicitly assuming that whatever movements in sales volumes are

---

[7] SKU: stock keeping unit
[8] MRO: maintenance, repair, and operation

Table 4.2 Financial impact of price adjustments

Price	Volume	Price elasticity	Revenue	Cost	Profit
100	100	–	10,000	9,000	1,000
105	100	0	10,500	9,000	1,500
110	95	-0.5	10,450	8,550	1,900
120	80	-1.0	9,600	7,200	2,400
130	75	-0.8	9,750	6,750	3,000

Marginal cost remains constant at 90

triggered and influenced solely by price changes. Unfortunately, it is safe to assume that this assumption does not always hold. Sales volumes would fluctuate, for example, due to seasonality without anything to do with pricing. Any unforeseen event would become noise in sorting out the correlation between price change and volume change—it is a challenge that just cannot be solved neatly. While market events are force majeure, competitive reactions may be anticipated and analyzed to a certain extent. However, the price elasticity diagnosis based on historical data will never ever become a white box.

Product managers and pricing practitioners should be prepared to deal with uncertainty. One effective way to triangulate price elasticities from historical data is to conduct market research. The methods to discover willingness to pay in Sect. 3.3 can be used to derive price elasticities. Take the Pricing Sandbox as an example. Recall Fig. 3.6, which is reminiscent of Fig. 4.4—both are concerned with the question—what will happen to the sales volume if we change the price. The former is based on expert opinions, and the latter is based on historical data. It is ideal to marry both. The results of price changes in the past serve as a good starting point for discussion during the Pricing Sandbox exercise. We are most interested in the circumstances under which the past price decisions were made and the variables that impacted the outcome. A solid understanding of past events would remarkably improve the quality of the price-response estimation at present.

Notably, one thing that we are not able to read off historical data analysis is the competitive reaction, which is a *Factor X* that has a significant impact on the price decisions we take. If all major competitors follow suit with our price adjustments, then we will benefit in a price increase situation but suffer in a price decrease situation for a simple reason, namely, competitive reaction is a regulator to our own pricing maneuvers. A good understanding of competitive behavior plays a critical role in pricing decisions.

From a methodological point of view, a conjoint-based model is ideal for simulating the impact of shifts in customer preferences and for wargaming competitive reactions. With the help of conjoint analysis, we can reconstruct the demand curve, articulating price elasticities in virtually all scenarios with varying value and price combinations. Unfortunately, the hurdles in applying conjoint analysis are high, as explained in Sect. 3.3.4.

When using price elasticities to inform pricing decisions, we need to keep in mind that price elasticity is extremely sensitive to conditions such as:

- **Price level**. Recall Fig. 4.3. At different price levels, price elasticities may differ, especially when surpassing a price threshold.
- **Customers' reaction**. Price elasticity is an aggregate concept. Different customer groups may react differently to the same price change, which speaks for consideration of differentiated price moves for different customer groups.
- **Competitors' reaction**. As discussed above, competitors will have a significant impact on price elasticity. If competitors follow suit with your price changes, price elasticities will be neutralized to zero. It is extremely harmful when you are launching a price promotion in the hope of boosting sales.
- **Communication**. Price promotions need to be heard by customers to reach their full potential in a timely fashion. In the meantime, we want to stay out of the radar of our competitors. It is a fine balance.

Finally, we have only talked about "straight" price elasticity up to this point. There is another type of price elasticity called *cross-price elasticity*.

Cross-price elasticity measures the responsiveness in the quantity demanded of *one* product when the price of *another* product changes. It is highly relevant if you have a product portfolio with substitutable products.

Imagine you are the owner of a bistro. When you increase the price of curried sausages from 4 to 4.5 EUR, the sales volume dips as a result. However, it is not the whole story. Customers who are upset by the price increase for curried sausages have two choices.

Choice 1: they will go somewhere else.
Choice 2: they will buy something else, such as the 5 EUR hamburger, which appears more attractive considering the price increase of curried sausages.

Hypothetically speaking, a 10% increase in the sales volume of hamburgers following a 12.5% price increase of curried sausages suggests a cross-price elasticity of 0.8. Note that cross-price elasticities are usually positive. As the example above shows, cross-price elasticities can be obtained and applied the same way as price elasticities. Therefore, I will leave it at that.

4.5 Summary

- Customers' needs tend to change and diversify over time.
- Regular updates of customer profiles are beneficial for achieving better financial results, as they could reduce customer churn which usually originates from dissatisfactory products or poor shopping experiences.
- There are four common variants of customer profiling, namely, demographic profiling, geographic profiling, psychographic profiling, and behavioral profiling.
- To be able to act on customer profiling, we need to determine whether different use cases have emerged because use cases tell us about customers' value perception and, in turn, their willingness to pay—it is what matters in the end.

- A use case can be characterized in three aspects, insights of which allude to concrete actions to be taken.

  - **The core**: what features about the product do customers like or dislike?
  - **The rationale**: what problems does the customer want to solve?
  - **The journey**: how do customers inform themselves about the product? Where do they shop? Who else would influence their purchase decisions?

- Over time, as the product becomes more sophisticated to keep abreast of diversifying customer needs, pricing also needs to evolve toward a higher level of differentiation.
- Price differentiation bears a risk, namely, price contamination. Companies should build barriers (fencing) to encourage a customer to stay in a higher-end option or discourage them to move down to a lower-end option, or both.
- There are three different fences at work.

  - **The good**: a good fence relies on customers' self-selection with little intervention required from the seller, making it the most customer-friendly type of fence possible.
  - **The bad**: fences are bad for customers when it takes time and effort to get around. They incur opportunity costs for customers.
  - **The ugly**: things get ugly when it hurts the customer to cross the fence, as the seller takes extreme measures to make customers stay clear of the fence.

- The incremental profit will decrease with the degree of price differentiation. Fencing comes at a cost. This implies that there must be an optimal level of price differentiation.
- Price elasticity is a particularly important concept for price management. If you know your price elasticity and cost information, you can nail down the price that results in profit optimum.
- Price elasticity tells us by how many percentage points more products will be sold (either through more buying customers or when more

products are sold per customer, or both), if the seller reduces the price by a percentage point, or vice versa.
- Price elasticity is fluid, like water. There are at least three types of demand curves with different implications for price elasticities (Fig. 4.3).
- A universal price elasticity databank does not exist, nor will it help you. You must curate your own price elasticity knowledge over time.
- To calculate price elasticities, we can conduct historical data analysis complete with market research methods as introduced in Chap. 3.
- Cross-price elasticity measures the responsiveness in the quantity demanded of one product when the price of another product changes. It is highly relevant if you have a product portfolio with substitutable products.

5

Maneuver Shades of Pricing

The business continues to grow. In the meantime, price management becomes increasingly complex. There are a few pricing topics which require special attention from the management.

5.1 How to Navigate Complexity

In the fledging days, pricing is about realizing the product-market-price fit (see Fig. 3.2) in the first place. Entering a more mature stage, the company will find itself with a more complicated product portfolio paired with a more diversified customer base. As a result, more pricing decisions need to be made and more price points need to be trimmed on a regular basis.

Without proper maintenance, pricing is on a trajectory to get out of hand. It is not only reflected in an oversimplified pricing process. Mismanagement of pricing also manifests itself in the results.

5.1.1 ABCD Analysis

We can use ABCD analysis to get a sense of current price quality. The ABCD analysis has its origins in inventory management. The letters A, B, C, and D correspond to the products' decreasing importance in terms of revenue contribution.

The classification is performed in two steps. In the first step, we sort the products by revenue in the last 12 months (alternative periods are also possible). Consider a simple spreadsheet with four columns: product ID, product name, product revenue, and product revenue share as a percentage of total revenue.

In the second step, we insert a fifth column to calculate accumulated revenue share per row. All products with an accumulated revenue share no greater than 50% are categorized as "A," the next 25% will be "B," the next 20% will be "C," and the remaining products at the bottom will fall in the category "D." Figure 5.1 depicts the ABCD analysis as shown below.

By including cost information in the ABCD analysis, we can gain additional insights. Table 5.1 showcases an exemplary case.

Table 5.1 provides a snapshot of a few key indicators by category. By design, the revenue shares are 50%, 25%, 20%, and 5% for the **four** categories. The percentages of SKUs that belong to each category are intuitive, where an 80–20 rule roughly applies. We can find hints about the price quality in the last two columns. Product categories A and B

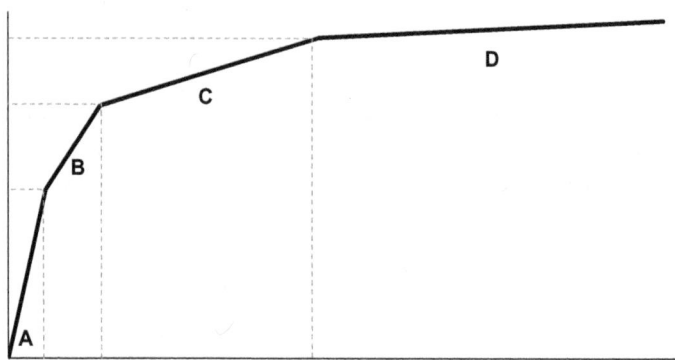

Fig. 5.1 ABCD analysis

Table 5.1 ABCD deep-dive

	% Revenue	% SKU	Average profit margin (%)
A	50	5	31
B	25	10	29
C	20	25	30
D	5	60	30

Table 5.2 Price engineering based on ABCD analysis

	% Revenue	% SKU	Average profit margin (%) - Old -	Price increase in %	Average profit margin (%) - New -
A	50	5	31	0	31
B	25	10	29	4	32
C	20	25	30	5	33
D	5	60	30	8	35
Weighted average			30	2.4	32

are fast-moving and are expected to be confronted with fiercer competition, while product categories C and D can be thought of as longtail products, which have lower visibility in the market and consequently less competition pressure. If there is no significant difference in cost structure among competitors, product categories C and D are expected to contribute a higher profit margin, which is obviously not the case here. Something is off. There is probably money left on the table, as we expect increasing margins from high-turnover products moving to longtail products.

The impact of price fine-tuning is illustrated through a simple back of the napkin calculation. In the current situation, the weighted average percentage profit margin is 30%. If we raise the prices of product categories B through D while leaving A's untouched, we will be able to improve the overall profit margin to approximately 32%. See the comparison in Table 5.2.

Although the price increase is not risk-free, it is worth trying, as we are only touching on products that are drifting at the perimeters of customers' and competitors' radars. The financial payback is sizable. If the business is making an annual revenue of $100 million, the price adjustment will result in a return of $2.4 million with limited efforts.

The logic of a product ABCD analysis would apply to a customer ABCD analysis analogically, should the company sell rather homogenous products to heterogenous customer groups. It is reasonable to assume that "A" customers should account for a large share of revenue with a lower percentage profit margin, whereas "D" customers contribute a higher percentage profit margin despite lower revenue.

5.1.2 Systematic Product Categorization

ABCD analysis reveals pricing inconsistencies and can allude to an immediate solution as illustrated in Table 5.2. To ensure pricing quality going forward, we need to establish a foundation for more coherent price management, namely, a systematic product categorization, based on which different pricing rules should be applied.

Figure 5.2 summarizes a typical type of product categorization, which divides the product portfolio into three categories, i.e., focus products, flagship products, and longtail products.

Focus products have the highest visibility in the market. Customers frequently buy them and have a good knowledge of both price (changes) and available alternatives from various competing brands.

Therefore, both customers and competitors will watch the prices of focus products very closely. Focus products often serve as traffic drivers, which play a significant role in acquiring new customers and creating cross-selling opportunities with existing customers.

PRODUCT CATEGORY	Focus Products	Flagship Products	Longtail Products
PRICING ROLE	Maintaining price image and driving traffic	Uphold value proposition while maintaining healthy profitability	Ensure sufficient profitability
PRICING APPROACH	Competition oriented	Value driven	Algorithm based
UPDATE FREQUENCY	Frequently	Regularly	Regularly

Fig. 5.2 Pricing by category

Pricing of focus products is closely pegged to competitors with the aim of maintaining a narrow price corridor to stay attractive to customers. Depending on customers' value perception, focus products can be more or less expensive than competitors' products or be the same. The desired brand/price positioning also plays a role here.

Price updates of the focus products will be conducted frequently. The intervals depend to a substantial extent on the market environment in which the company operates. The sky is the limit. Amazon, for example, would make over 250 million price changes every day. The average product's price will change once every 10 min (Curling-Hope, 2022). It should be noted that frequent pricing fluctuations do not guarantee greater financial success.

Flagship products carry something unique that is not easy for your competitors to copy, be it a product feature, or simply aesthetic appeal. This results in greater freedom in pricing. Here, the golden principle applies, namely, price should be closely aligned with value. A healthy percentage profit margin is expected so that you can finance your market operations and R&D.

The pricing of flagship products is less dependent on competitors due to a lack of perfect substitutes. Value-based pricing should prevail. That said, close monitoring of competitors is indispensable, especially regarding new product development. A shift in customers' preferences will have a major impact on product design and pricing.

Price updates of flagship products should be performed regularly in the form of a price audit at least once a year, if not more frequently. If price is aligned with customers' value perception and there are no considerable cost changes, then it is not imperative to change prices.

Longtail products would receive least attention from all sides—customers, competitors, and you yourself. Longtail constitutes only a small share of revenue for the company and is often "logically" deprioritized in price management, if not ignored at all. The truth is that longtail products are a treasure chest for profits. Take the automotive industry as an example. Both carmakers and the third-party dealers struggle with making money on new car sales, as the competition becomes fiercer and fiercer. The modern passenger car business increasingly resembles the printer business, where the manufacturers make money primarily on consumables i.e., inkjet cartridges, rather than on durables i.e., printers.

Indeed, carmakers and dealers rely heavily on the aftersales business to turn a profit. Among spare parts, maintenance, and wear parts such as oil filters, air filters, and tires are heavyweights in revenue contribution, while the competition is so harsh that the profit margin is under enormous pressure all the time. These are focus products for which the pricing leeway is extremely limited. Profit potential stems rather from longtail products, which customers are not knowledgeable about because of limited shopping experience and lack of alternative offers. It is common that longtail products have an absurd profit margin north of 50%.

The No. 1 pricing challenge with longtail products is that it is beyond the limits of active manual management due to the formidable number of SKUs to be managed. It calls for enaction of a pricing algorithm, which automates the pricing of longtail products following certain preset rules including but not limited to minimum margin requirement, target price premium or discount versus a pre-specified competitive basket. There is plenty of pricing software for longtail product pricing on the market currently. A word of caution is deemed necessary: software is an immense help in achieving your goals; however, it cannot and should not define the goals for you.

Now, you might wonder how you can categorize focus, flagship, and longtail products. It is a good question to which I hesitate to answer thus far because there is no perfect answer. However, the good news is that it is not rocket science, where common sense does help.

Focus products are those that lead in turnover frequency. The higher the turnover ratio is, the more likely it is that the product will qualify as a focus product. Flagship products should present themselves naturally. After all, they should build the bed stone of the business, whose identification should be a no-brainer. Otherwise, we will have a much larger problem, namely, what we (want to) stand for.

While focus and flagship products are mainly found in product categories A and B, longtail products most likely coincide with C and D products, following the terminology of the ABCD analysis. They have a much lower turnover frequency. Fewer customers would buy them and have fewer alternative products from competitors to compare with.

5.2 How to Improve Promotions

In the piece "*The Burden of Fame*" in my other book "*The Pricing Puzzle*" I expressed my empathy with an unwitting brand that was often significantly discounted at grocery stores. It is detrimental to the image of a premium brand; customers may not appreciate it because the promotion has become more of a routine; the worst of all being the promotion initiator, the retailer does not benefit from the promotion in the absence of incremental profit.

The reality is that promotions are prevalent everywhere, as companies hope to spur sales with the help of promotions. Recall our discussion on price elasticity in the last chapter: if all competitors are offering discounts, price cuts will not lead to additional sales volumes, as customers take them for granted. Gradually, promotions hold hostage companies across many different verticals.

While promotions could still make sense in the B2C sector, it is generally a bad idea for industrial companies to engage with price promotions. Consumers will buy stuff on the spur of the moment, although they may regret it afterward. In the manufacturing industry, the demand is foreseeably stable in the short- to mid-term. This means that in contrast to consumer goods, promotions for industrial goods result in stock-ups, which is bad for business eventually: today's sales are increased at the expense of future sales. It is value-destroying from an NPV[1] perspective. In effect, the discount rate in the period assumed in the NPV calculation is substituted by the percentage of cash discounts granted to customers today. In most cases, the latter is significantly higher than the former, resulting in a lower NPV—detrimental to the enterprise value. Period. Manufacturing companies should really stay away from promotions, which should remain first and foremost a headache for retailers.

You might have heard that promotions could serve many different purposes, such as attracting new customers, increasing revenue, increasing store traffic, generating more profit, rewarding customer loyalty, eliminating obsolete stock, and so on.

---

[1] NPV: net present value, which equals to the sum of all future cash flows over the investment's lifetime, discounted to the present value.

All sounds legitimate. Some goals are short-term, others are rather long-term; some goals are tangible, and others are less so. Regardless of the goal, the ultimate criterion for evaluating a promotion should be whether it helps the company make more profit. However, it is exceedingly difficult to judge whether this is the case because there are so many factors that can influence the outcome of a promotion. Many retailers struggle with separating incremental sales from total sales realized in a promotion, not to mention the real incremental profit through the promotion.

The challenge already begins with determining the baseline revenue that would have been realized without the respective promotion. While the exact number may remain elusive, an educated guesstimate based on historical data should be possible. Incremental revenue is then what comes on top of the baseline revenue during the promotion.

The quantification of incremental profit is much more complicated and requires a range of inputs including promotion spends including actual discounts and ad costs, supplier funding, cannibalization as well as cross-selling effects within the product portfolio (recall cross-price elasticity in Sect. 4.4.4!), loss of future sales due to promotion-induced hoarding, extra logistics and overhead expenses, etc. While the advancement of technology in analytics is easing pain, it will be naive to believe that there will be a promotion crystal ball that can tell us everything—a certain level of uncertainty will persist.

Despite all the ranting above, we must accept the fact that promotions play an integral part in any retail business in the present day, whether we (or I) like it or not. Therefore, the real question to be answered is how we can get the best out of it, which can be broken down into three parts, namely, who is eligible for promotions, what products are suitable for promotions, and how to design effective promotions. It must be noted that the following elaboration centers on promotions with the goal of boosting sales and profit. Markdowns, clearance sales, and others that pursue other goals are excluded from the scope of discussion. Without further due, let us start with the who.

5.2.1 Who Is Eligible for Promotions

We like customers to spend more. If promotions can trigger customers to do so, there is a positive ROI[2] case. Therefore, it is of utmost importance to think through who we want to target in promotions.

Customers can be categorized along two dimensions in a simple 2 × 2 matrix (see the illustration in Fig. 5.3), the two dimensions being shopper type and budget. Loyal shoppers tend to stick to one retailer as their go-to place. In contrast, smart shoppers are on the watch for alternatives. They have a list of preferred retailers in mind, possibly organized by product category. A shift in the value-price equation of the alternative would trigger a change in their shopping routine.

The spending budget serves as a proxy for price sensitivity. Affluent customers tend to have a higher budget coupled with a lower price sensitivity. On the other hand, financially constrained customers usually shop on a lower budget and are more sensitive to price changes.

Smart shoppers with a high budget are most promising for generating a positive ROI in promotions. We would also consider loyal customers with a high budget as the target group of promotions if they were enticed to try out something new in our product portfolio.

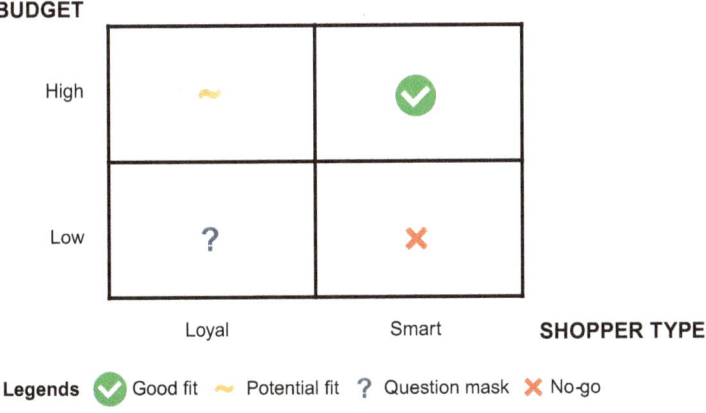

Fig. 5.3 Get the best of promotion—who?

---
[2] ROI: return on investment

In the meantime, I have less faith in loyal customers with a low budget. Even if they like to spend, the upside sales potential is somewhat limited. More importantly, I believe that promotions should not target the last customer group, i.e., the smart shoppers with a limited budget. They are and will always be sitting on the fence, ready to jump ship by finding the next best viable option in the market. The chance is slim that we can convert them into loyal customers or get them into buying additional items outside promotions. The best advice I can give is to stay away from them to minimize waste.

To choose who we want to admit to promotions, we need an identification and attribution process. Identification concerns about profiling and assigning customers to the cells in the matrix. Attribution is arguably more challenging, as we need to grant/deny certain customer groups access to promotions. A certain kind of differentiation and fencing is needed.

The German grocery retailer Lidl provides us with a good example. Its Lidl Plus Loyalty Program allows customers to collect coupons whenever they make a purchase. These coupons are collected and must be redeemed before expiration within a few days. In this mechanism by design, smart customers with a high budget will be most rewarded. The more they shop there, the more they will become reliant on the retailer. This all will work if the customers believe that they are being treated fairly. Remember that smart shoppers always keep looking for good deals.

5.2.2 What Products Are Suitable for Promotions

What kind of products a retailer chooses to put on promotion would make a significant difference in the outcome. We can look at this from the perspective of the customer and that of the retailer.

The customers will find a well-known national or international brand more palatable; the retailer, on the other hand, will like to increase the likelihood of a positive payout—the higher margin the promoted has, the bigger the odds that the retailer will generate a positive ROI on the promotion. The impact of these two perspectives on the "what" question for promotion is reflected in Fig. 5.4.

Fig. 5.4 Get the best of promotion—what?

The common ground is to be found in the first quadrant (the top right cell in the matrix), where the retailer manages to offer a branded product to the customer while generating a positive monetary impact. However, we all know that things do not always come our way. At times, retailers must head south to the second quadrant (the bottom right cell in the matrix) to consider products with high brand awareness but low margins for promotions, the reason usually being that the brand in question has such a strong appeal that it is worth making a loss on the promoted product in the hope for increased sales of other items to be put in the shopping cart.

The promoted products in this calculated loss-making strategy are called "loss leaders.[3]" Grocery stores frequently use products such as pasta, coffee, beverages, and snacks as loss leaders since they are popular, essential products. Knowing what these items usually cost, the shoppers will feel rewarded thanks to the promotion and are more likely to add other items into the shopping basket.

This would explain why leading German food (and actually non-food as well) retailers such as REWE and Lidl would heavily discount

---

[3] Loss leader definition: a loss leader is a pricing strategy where a product is sold at a price below its market cost to stimulate other sales of more profitable goods or services. With this sales promotion/marketing strategy, a "leader" is any popular article, i.e., sold at a low price to attract customers (Wikipedia, 2023g).

brands such as Barilla (Italian pasta) and Pringles (potato-based chips[4]) on a recurring basis. REWE and Co. deliberately use well-known brands as loss leaders to incentivize patrons to check in the store more frequently. It comes down to perception management. If customers believe that good deals await them at a certain grocery store, their loyalty to the store increases. This kind of benefit from promotions was hard to measure in the past. Thanks to today's widespread digital footprint, it has become at least technologically possible to track it down.

Sometimes suppliers will subsidize promotions, especially when they attempt to gain more market shares from competitors. In such cases, products that originally fall in the second quadrant will eventually move up to the first quadrant, a win–win situation for both the retailer and the customer. The supplier tends to regard the promotion fund as marketing dollars (investment) instead of outright discounts (expenses). In this light, funding a promotion is also less painful for the supplier.

It would be a different story, if the supplier participating in the promotion is a less-known brand. The problem is that we know the promoted products will likely make a loss on a stand-alone basis. In the case of a less-known brand, the sacrifice will probably not trigger incremental sale of other items. As a result, these products are not *loss leaders*; they are *loss losers*. Losers do not attract customers; they alienate customers instead. It is not a promising idea, especially when the products in question are already lingering in a low profit zone.

Following the logic of ABCD analysis (see Fig. 5.1 and Table 5.1), product categories A and B are good candidates for promotion. It is generally a bad idea to put product categories C and D on promotion.

To conclude, promotion is a race. There are two main criteria for the qualification of a product to be enlisted in promotion: it must be a well-known, enticing brand, and it should be backed up by a good margin or supplier financing. After identifying target customers and products, we now continue to discuss how we can design an effective promotion.

---

[4] For those who might be interested, Pringles are not really potato chips (Mueller, 2021).

5.2.3 How to Design Effective Promotions

Promotional design is a challenging task. There are experts who specialize solely in promotion. On a high level, for promotions to be effective, one must have a solid understanding of the customer segments being targeted and the goals being pursued. A good promotion strategy, like pricing, should be segmented and tailored to the peculiarities of each segment, including but not limited to product preferences, shopping budgets, information channels, and so on. Obviously, how to design effective promotions is a complicated topic. To keep things simple, I choose to focus on the two most important aspects of promotion design here.

The first aspect is complexity. It is beyond the imagination of an average consumer as to how complex promotions can become. A sophisticated pricing team at a well-established consumer goods company was creative enough to devise 12 different types of promotions: price discounts, BOGO,[5] free samples, multipacks, coupons, gift points, just to name a few.

It is already becoming difficult to have a good grasp of all these promotions. However, the complexity does not end here. Remember I touched upon the importance of differentiation by segment? The resourceful pricing team here aced it by identifying eight different customer segments, each of which manifested certain preferences for different promotions. Although not all promotion types apply to all segments, we end up with over 80 different promotions. This is merely the fundament of promotional campaigns, as different products and communication channels need to be determined for each promotion. On critical shopping occasions during the year, some special promotions need to be crafted in addition.

If you have multiple promotions running at the same time, it can become exceedingly messy. Without superior analytical prowess, it may end in a lose–lose situation—the customer becomes confused or even irritated by the promotion chaos; the retailer loses control over everything—they do not know what happened; they do not know how it happened; they can only wonder. Not knowing bodes badly for a business.

---

[5] BOGO: buy one, get one

Take the infamous Double 11 promotion fiesta in China as an example. Alibaba invented Double 11 as a tribute to Black Friday in the USA. The former soon outshined the latter in terms of GMV[6] and impact on consumers' shopping behavior. As the name suggests, Double 11 is a man-made shopping festival whose main date is 11 November every year. The time window of the grand shopping gala opens roughly a month in advance, kicking off the presales season. There are overly complex rules as to how a consumer can combine different promotions granted by the e-commerce platform and merchants to get the most out of it. There is a joke that one must be exceptionally good at math to figure out the best deal in total in the Double 11 shopping competition.

The complexity holds everyone hostage: the e-commerce behemoths and archenemies Taobao and JD.com would force merchants to participate in shopping festivals (yes, the plural form is intended, since there are several large promotions days besides Double 11 in the year), where participating is intended as a euphemism for providing funds for promotions. Merchants are forced to play along, as the rule *"in or out"* applies—"in" as in participating in various promotional campaigns, and "out" as in being delisted from the platform. It is a high-stakes decision to be made. Meanwhile, consumers are so overwhelmed that the promotions are perceived more as a burden than joy. The efforts to be part of promotions have become just unbearable.

I am a huge fan of the *KISS* principle, which stands for *"Keep it simple, stupid."* It is a design principle first noted by the US Navy in 1960. The KISS principle states that most systems work best if they are kept simple rather than made complicated; therefore, simplicity should be a key design principle, and unnecessary complexity should be avoided (Wikipedia, 2023f). Simplicity is good for everybody—easy to understand, easy to participate, easy to evaluate… Complexity appears sophisticated. However, it is not necessarily superior. My take on promotions is

---

[6] GMV: gross merchandise volume. It is a term used in online retailing to indicate a total sale monetary value (e.g., in US dollars or Euros) for merchandise sold through a particular marketplace over a certain time frame. GMV includes any fees or other deductions which a seller might calculate separately. Site revenue comes from fees and is different from the monetary value of items sold (Wikipedia, 2023d).

that the promotion strategy should be as complex as needed and as simple as possible.

Coming back to the promotion chaos at Double 11 and alike. The race for creativeness in promotions plateaued in 2019, when complaints of frustrated customers soared. Even the state media covered the story and called for rethinking the overcomplicated approach to promotions. Since then, things have cooled down considerably. In the meantime, savvy consumers have discovered that many merchants would raise list prices prior to large promotional campaigns to compensate for imminent price cuts. Therefore, there is no actual gain despite all the stress in partaking in the promotion game.

The second aspect of promotion design has to do with timing. If you call on any marketing team of sizable consumer goods companies in China, I bet all of them can show you a promotion calendar listing all promotion plans during a year. Guess which month is promotion-free. The 13th month.[7]

Let us have a rundown of the promotional calendar. The annual promotion calendar would start with New Year in January. February has St. Valentine's and Chinese New Year most of time (following a lunar calendar, Chinese New Year may occur in January as well); March has International Women's Day; April has Qing Ming (a spring festival in China when graves are put in order and special offerings are made to the dead); May features Labor Day and the Golden Week; June is a very crowded month hosting Children's Day, Dragon Boat Festival, Father's Day, National College Entrance Examination (gifting and celebrations are common after the national exam), and last, the heavy-weight 618 Shopping Festival (one of the two most shopping festivals alongside Double 11). July and August are good for tourism and shopping, as students enjoy their summer vacation. The highlight in the summer is the Qixi Festival or Double 7 Festival as it is observed on the 7th day of the 7th lunar month. Youngsters crave it as the Chinese Valentine's Day. September celebrates Teacher's Day and Mid-autumn Festival (also known as the mooncake festival). October is also busy with National Day Holidays, Chongyang Festival, also known as Double 9 Festival (observed

---

[7] According to the lunar calendar, the 13th month does occur 7 out of every 19 years.

on the ninth of the ninth lunar month, a day to show appreciation for the elderly). Recently, the younger generation of Chinese have also picked up Halloween and Thanksgiving, which have October and November covered. The largest promotion event in a year is undoubtedly the Double 11 Festival in November. In the last month of the year, Chinese celebrate Winter Solstice, while many young people celebrate Christmas with their beloved ones and bid farewell to a well-spent year.

Less prominent shopping occasions have not yet been included in the list above. You can imagine how busy a marketer can get by planning promotions "only" for the important occasions. If every retailer is going to run the promotions according to the promotion calendar, the attractiveness of promotions wanes, if not, drains.

The abundance of promotions brings about two negative consequences for the retailer. First, promotions no longer stimulate demand; second, the price tag loses its touch with value signaling, as consumers are primed to pay more attention to the promoted price, i.e., the "real" price which may vary across promotions. Therefore, the whole idea of promoting collapses in the presence of predictable, regular promotions.

Why do companies keep doing promotions? In my opinion, lack of means to differentiate from competitors is a cardinal reason. Not following suit with me-too competitors on promotions risks losing needed exposure to retain customers and revenue. However, in the end, it is a level playing field, in which a low price alone cannot be a sustainable strategy. To survive in the long run, companies must be better and more innovative than competitors, not only in price but also in value.

Amazon's *Subscribe and Save* is a nice example of transforming ordinary promotions into something extraordinary. By setting up regularly scheduled deliveries, customers earn savings with *Subscribe & Save*. From diapers to toothpaste to dog treats, customers can subscribe to thousands of everyday products. Savings amount up to 15% when receiving 5 or more products in one auto-delivery to one address. In advance of each delivery, Amazon will send the subscriber a reminder email showing the items, price, and any applicable discount for the upcoming delivery. The price of the item may decrease or increase from delivery to delivery, depending on the Amazon.com price of the item at the time of the order processing. The subscriptions can be changed or canceled any time (Amazon, 2023).

The subscription process is smooth and carefree. There are allegedly no hidden costs. The price is transparent. Customers are assured that they are in control, which is also true. The subscribe & save routine forms a habit loop that reinforces the customer's good feelings. This is the *Power of Habit*. For those who are interested in the topic, the namesake book by Charles Duhigg is highly recommendable. Chances are that Amazon's "Subscribe and Save" does not create extra demand. However, by reserving customers' future demand, Amazon effectively staves off competition. Figure 5.5 depicts the discussion around effective promotion design.

With the goal of boosting revenue and profit in mind, the first quadrant of simple sporadic promotions would be most beneficial for the retailer. Amazon's "Subscribe and Save" falls in the fourth quadrant (the top left corner in the matrix). I like the simplicity. However, the regularity would eventually limit its impact on revenue and profit.

Before we move on the next topic, I would like to briefly touch on one tricky question in promotion design, namely, how much incentive is needed for a promotion to be effective? Simply put, how much discount should a retailer give away?

The short answer is that the perceived value matters more than the actual discount. You will find more clues in Sect. 5.7, which delves into consumer psychology and its impact on pricing including promotion pricing. However, as a rule of thumb, customers do not get happier after

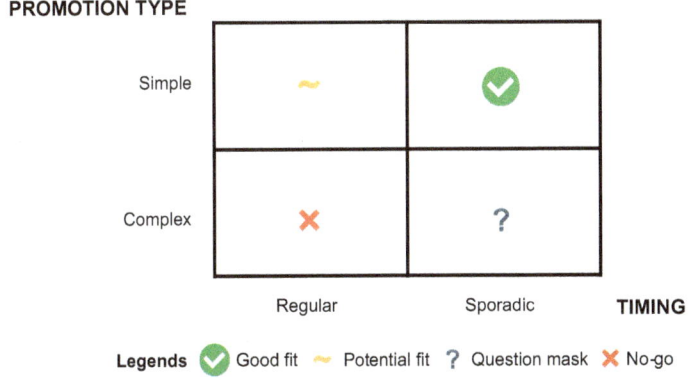

Fig. 5.5 Get the best of promotion—how?

the price reduction exceeds a certain threshold. Based on my experience, the joy of receiving a discount typically begins to wear off at approximately 30%. The law of diminishing returns applies. Too large a discount would also trigger concern over the quality of the brand and the pricing integrity of the retailer.

5.3 How to Manage Distribution

5.3.1 Is Distribution Outdated?

Direct sale is the zeitgeist of our time. Tesla mastered the direct selling model and was a breath of fresh air, when powerhouses such as General Motors, Toyota, and Volkswagen had relied on independently owned dealerships for decades to sell and provide aftersales service to their customers.

Tesla is now by far the largest carmaker in the world by market cap. The second largest is Toyota, whose market cap is less than one third that of Tesla. General Motors and Volkswagen combined would be worth one seventh of Tesla in September 2023 (Yahoo Finance, 2023).

The success story of Tesla is attributed in part to its unique direct selling model, which allows Tesla to engage with customers directly and gather information firsthand. Chinese EV upstarts such as Nio, XPeng, and Li Auto followed in its footsteps and adopted a similar direct selling model.

As time went by, established players were pressured to test the water with new sales models. In 2020, Volkswagen launched the so-called agency model, in which customers order directly from the manufacturer, and the dealer only acts as an intermediary agent. The Wolfsburg-based carmaker announced at its European dealer congress in 2021 that the sales model would be significantly expanded (Randall, 2021). From a pricing perspective, the agency model is remarkably similar to direct sale in that the manufacturer can set the retail price and the dealers earn a fixed percentage commission based on car model.

While the entirety of the automotive industry seemed ready to embrace the direct selling model, XPeng announced in September

2023 to gradually replace its direct stores with dealer shops. He Xiaopeng, the EV maker's chairperson and CEO, said in an analyst call following the second-quarter earnings report in 2023 that Xpeng will recruit partners at a faster pace to accelerate market share expansion in second-tier and lower-tier cities in the people's republic of China. Dealers have rich channel resources and flexible store-building capital, which can help XPeng reduce the financial and operational burden of managing its own stores and quickly expand in lower-tier markets (Zhang, 2023).

XPeng was not the only one who changed gears. Nio and Geely's EV brand Zeekr announced plans around the same time to partner with independently owned dealerships to accelerate growth outside of China's metropolitan areas. When Chinese automakers entered European markets, they often partnered with local dealer groups. XPeng and Great Wall Motor, for example, formed a strategic partnership with Emil Frey, Europe's largest car dealer group.

The debate over direct sales vs. third-party distribution has not yet been settled. A realistic scenario is that both sales models will continue to coexist in the near future, not only in the automotive industry but also elsewhere. Direct selling shortens the communication circle between manufacturers and customers, allowing the former to react faster and have better control over brand image and pricing, among others. Third-party distribution, on the other hand, saves the manufacturer time and money while allowing for faster growth.

As direct sale is no different from B2C retailing from a pricing perspective, we will focus on distribution pricing in what follows. In a distribution sales model, manufacturers are legally forbidden to dictate the retail price in most countries. Instead, they can only recommend the retail price, which is called the manufacturer's suggested retail price, or MSRP in short.

Distributors serve as an extended arm of manufacturers and play a significant role in everything that has to do with the end customers, including selling, maintaining customer relationships, managing deliveries, price setting and negotiations.

5.3.2 Managing Distribution from a Pricing Perspective

Managing distributors is not easy, especially when a manufacturer works with a variety of distributors to cover different channels or regions. Often, there are conflicts of interest between the manufacturer and the distributors and among different distributors. At the end of the day, it all boils down to one ultimate question: how to divide the cake fairly? Pricing governance is a vital component of distribution management, which is not only supposed to make sure to divide the cake fairly, but also helps to make the cake larger.

Pricing governance in trade manifests itself primarily in the form of terms and conditions. A world's leading B2B electronics company has a sophisticated product portfolio that continues to grow. It has two main sales channels: the key accounts are managed by its direct sales team, while small-to-medium sized customers are serviced through distributors of varied sizes and maturity, which are spread out nationwide.

The management believes that they have good visibility on the key account business, as there are only a dozen large accounts with which they have been doing business for many years.

On the other hand, the availability of information on the small-to-medium sized clientele is not satisfactory. In fact, the management is very much reliant on the respective distributors to retrieve information, who differ by a large margin in terms of capability and willingness to cooperate.

For example, the electronics manufacturer suffers from limited pricing transparency among the variety of distributors, as the CRM system has not been installed until recently. At the same time, the sales VP remains optimistic about distributor price management and goes:

> I think we at least get 80% of it right.

Unfortunately, the data does not seem to support the 80% hypothesis. Figure 5.6 shows sanitized results of a data analysis. Each dot in the graph represents a distributor in a particular region. The purchase value on the *x*-axis is calculated as the accumulated net revenue that the electronics

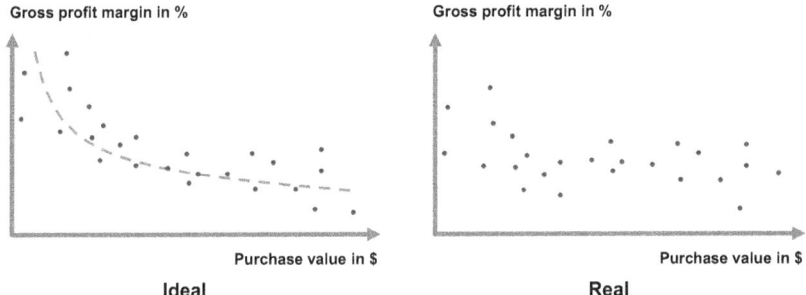

Fig. 5.6 The relationship between purchase value and gross profit margin

companies realized with the respective distributor in the last 12 months. Gross profit margin is calculated as the difference between net revenue and cost of goods sold divided by net revenue for each distributor.

The left part of Fig. 5.6 represents an ideal state, in which the distributors are largely rewarded according to the size of their revenue contribution despite a few outliers. It is almost too good to be true and not necessarily ideal, as the single-variable interpretation obviously does not capture all factors that could have affected the level of the gross profit margin. However, this would be, by and large, an 80% right outcome.

The right part of Fig. 5.6 reflects the reality, which is refreshing as well as embarrassing. The stars are apparently not aligned for the manufacturer. The gross margins are all over the place, and their relationship with purchase value is inexplicable. Looking at this, we would intuitively know that something might be off.

The manufacturer has been working with many of these distributors for a long time. Every pricing decision made in the past could be well grounded on a stand-alone basis, from the sales manager's viewpoint. However, every pricing decision needs to be tested from the company's perspective under the circumstances when the deal is made. In other words, to ensure pricing consistency, we need to break down silos to create a level playing field for all customers to monitor and maintain prices on a regular basis.

Analogous to gardening, the pricing results will likely be somewhat wild without regular maintenance and upgrades. Restoring order is time-consuming, costly, and frustrating for all stakeholders. Caution is advised when retouching (revamping would be too difficult and risky to implement in a brief time) any legacy distributor pricing systems. It is preferable to take small steps, ensuring that we have some evangelists before we proceed and do not drive everyone crazy in the process. However, it takes time. Therefore, the best time to deal with distributor pricing is when you plan to enlist the first batch of distributors: lay a solid groundwork, then build and extend over time, as the business grows, and the more distributors are recruited. The second-best time to work on distributor pricing is now.

5.3.3 The GBB Pricing Model

As pricing sophistication increases, the distribution pricing mode should evolve following a Good-Better-Best construct. See Fig. 5.7.

The inception of distribution pricing is good enough if it starts out with a price band, which refers to sellout prices that the distributors must pay for the goods received. The initial band width is usually based on the prevalent market convention and depends on the outcome of the negotiation with pilot distributors, who are willing to take a risk in undertaking this new venture. The band width would vary by a large margin by industry, region, and notably business model.

Even within the same industry, distributors may earn quite different margins with different manufacturers. An Apple reseller would earn much less on iPhones than a distributor selling Android smartphones. According to The Economic Times, the world's largest technology

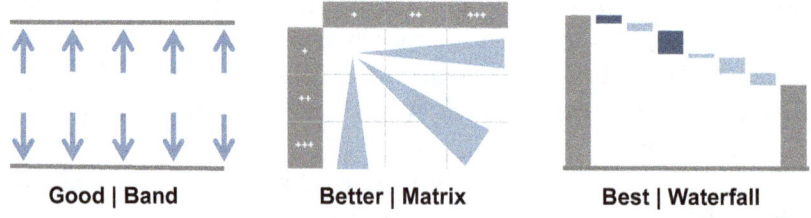

Fig. 5.7 Distributer pricing journey—the GBB model

company more than halved distributor margins on iPhones to 1.7–2.5% in 2018 (Kundu, 2018). The more unique the product is, the lower the profit margin the distributor is willing to accept, the reason being a unique product is more likely to bring in new customers and increase cross-selling opportunities. Accordingly, the manufacturer is in a better position to impose a low distributor margin, which aids in maintaining price consistency across channels.

The lower bound of the price band can be considered the cost of survival. In case the end customer is not ready to pay a price that is at least as high as the lower limit of the price band plus a minimum margin required from the distributor, the manufacturer should revisit its distribution model and reconsider other options, e.g., Are there alternative channels? Would direct sales be feasible?

The upper bound of the price band is the manufacturer's chance at the pricing alpha, a reward for extraordinary performance relative to competitors. It can be revealed through a trial-and-error process if the company does not discover it in the first place. If some smart distributors are found to sell the product at a higher price than the MSRP, it indicates that the product is in demand, in other words, underpriced. Price elevation, as the phenomenon is called in practice, suggests that the manufacturer has left money on the table and should consider taking corrective actions, namely, increasing the sellout price to distributors as well as the MSRP.

When sales expand, the manufacturer is set to enlist more distributors to facilitate growth. In tandem, the pricing model needs to improve as the price band reaches its limit in accommodating an increasing number of distributors. The differences among the distributors and the resulting pricing implications will be better captured in a two-dimensional matrix, where the sellout prices or discounts are governed by two dimensions. What composes the dimensions is at the discretion of the manufacturer if it makes sense.

As Fig. 5.7 indicates, the more "+" are assigned to a distributor, the higher the discounts will apply. Let us look at an example. One manufacturer decides to use "customer value" and "competitive intensity" as the two dimensions in the price matrix. On the one hand, customer value is determined by a set of quantitative factors, including annual purchase value, years of cooperation, sales growth in the last 2 years, payment behavior, etc. It is intuitive to derive the comparative level of customer value based on the factors listed above. On the other hand, competitive intensity is related to specific product groups sold by distributors and is an indicator of the level of competition. The assessment of competitive intensity can be performed based on the concentration of market shares in the respective product market when the data quality is adequate. Alternatively, it can also be approximated by expert judgment, whose underlying assumptions need to be challenged and aligned within the organization. After required deliberation and number crunching, we arrive at the discount matrix shown in Table 5.3.

The applicable discounts fall in a range from 20 to 30%, trending higher from the top left corner down to the bottom right corner. The "+" sign indicates the level of customer value and competitive intensity, respectively. The basic idea behind the matrix is that if a distributor is more valuable and faces more fierce competition, it should receive a higher discount.

It may already occur to some creative minds that the same principle of the two-dimensional matrix can be extended to a three-dimensional cube, which structures distributor discounts along three different dimensions. While an average person might still make sense of a three-dimensional cube, anything beyond three dimensions would be graphically impractical and no longer intuitive.

What do we do if the number of distributors continues to grow, and we need to factor in more elements in deciding on the distributor price?

Table 5.3 Distributor discount matrix

		Customer value			
		+	++	+++	++++
Competitive intensity	+	20%	22%	24%	26%
	++	21%	23%	25%	27%
	+++	22%	24%	26%	28%
	++++	24%	26%	28%	30%

The answer is a price waterfall. Price waterfall is a popular visualization tool in price management that provides a good overview of all price determinants. It is also a universal tool that can be applied for both trade and retail. One distinct advantage of the price waterfall is being all-encompassing, as it can map not only discounts but also rebates.

Discounts and rebates are two essential constituents in distribution pricing and profit management. Both are meant primarily to boost sales; however, the working mechanism is different.

A discount is a direct deduction of the cost of a product at the time of purchase. Therefore, it usually appears on the invoice in each transaction. The most common type is a volume discount: The higher the volume the distributor purchases, the larger the discount. In contrast, a rebate is not granted on the spot. Instead, it will only be paid out at intervals, usually at the end of a quarter or a year, provided that certain requirements such as revenue target or product mix target have been met in the current period. While discounts are normally simple and straightforward, rebates can become painstakingly specific and complex. Figure 5.8 highlights an example of price waterfall applied to two distributors A and B.

The first five price elements are paid out as discounts, meaning they are on the invoice. After subtracting the discounts, we arrive at the net price. After subtracting the last two price elements, which are off-the-invoice rebates, we will obtain the net net price—the way of writing is intended. The first rebate element is related to financial targets, namely, revenue growth; the second is meant to encourage compliance, which could have to do with ESG,[8] IT,[9] security, etc.

By design, the net net price, also known as 2N price, can only be calculated at the end of a financial period after the rebates have been paid out and serve as a measure of distributor performance.

We notice that both distributors A and B in Fig. 5.8 have a net net price that amounts to a 25% markdown from the list price. Although the results are the same, the underlying reasons are different. In Distributor A's case, the largest price driver is product mix, which means it has a favorable product portfolio that is line with the manufacturer's product

---

[8] ESG: environmental, social, and corporate governance
[9] IT: information technology

Fig. 5.8 Distributor price waterfall

strategy. Relatively speaking, Distributor B also does a decent job at product mix while scoring even better in marketing efforts.

The comparison of different distributors' price waterfalls sheds light on potential room for improvement. If Distributor A wants to make more money, it should work on marketing and payment. Distributor B should look for measures to improve performance in logistics and product mix.

5.3.4 Price Model Transition

Every time that you step up from an old terms and conditions system to a new one, there will be winners (those who benefit) and losers (those who become worse off) due to the paradigm change.

Obviously, it will be easier to convince the winners than the losers, as the way the winners do business remains unchanged. It is important for the manufacturer to socialize the changes beforehand, allowing time for those potential losers to take actions to preempt adverse results due to the introduction of the updated terms and conditions.

In an ideal scenario, at the end of the next budget year, some of the losers may emerge as winners and those original winners may win even bigger, as they jointly make the cake larger. There will still be losers, even big losers. These are candidates for elimination, which is not a dreadful thing for the manufacturer after all—just like how natural selection works. To build a stronger commercial ecosystem, we need stronger partners.

5.3.5 Discounts or Rebates

We touched upon the concepts of discounts and rebates previously, when introducing the distributor price waterfall. In fact, most manufacturers use both discounts and rebates to incentivize or reward their distributors.

Meanwhile, it can be quite a headache for the manufacturer to find the right ratio of discounts (*instant gratification* from the distributor's point of view) to rebates (*delayed gratification*). Both have their merits and demerits.

Let us look at two incentive schemes for comparison.

Scheme A: discounts outweigh rebates

Pros

1. It is distributor-friendly, as it improves the cash flow of the distributor.
2. It is easier to conduct financial planning for both the manufacturer and the distributor.

Cons

1. It will be more difficult for the manufacturer to manage price consistency across channels or parallel imports between countries, as the distributors have more leeway for reducing end customer prices, when they deem it necessary. This is part of the reason why Apple chooses to impose a low distributor margin.
2. The distributors have less incentive to go the extra mile to boost sales.

Scheme B: rebates outweigh discounts

Pros

1. It requires less upfront investment for the manufacturer.
2. It provides the distributors with a greater incentive to sell more to earn the reward.

Cons

1. It may give rise to faked demand toward year end, as distributors stock up/game the rules to qualify for higher annual bonuses, while there is also a risk of rental seeking.
2. The requirements for rebates can be complex and ambiguous, which leads to frustration and dissatisfaction of the distributors.

Overall, how to split between discounts and rebates remains at the discretion of each manufacturer, and there is no standard answer. In practice, discounts usually make up a larger proportion than rebates in the overall distributor compensation package. The share and size of rebates are subject to the strategic goals of the company and may vary over time.

Special caution is advised when a rebate element is linked to a financial target. The rules should be set in a way that they are not so easy to be gamed. For example, revenue-related bonuses at year end should not be paid in full amount until the Q1 sales figures have come in. By then, we should know whether the distributor has borrowed sales from the future. It will be a different story if it is in both the manufacturer's and the distributor's best interests to act differently. Finally, compliance-related rebates would come in handy to change distributors' behavior in following instructions.

5.4 How to Increase Prices

Price increases are unavoidable under circumstances, especially in an inflationary environment. Warren Buffet once commented on the relation between pricing power and price increases (Ray, 2019).

> "If you've got the power to raise prices without losing business to a competitor, you've got a very good business. And if you have to have a prayer session before raising the price by 10 percent, then you've got a terrible business."
>
> - Warren Buffett

I guess that most managers or business owners will have a prayer session before raising the price by 10%, as pricing power is a scarcity. This does not mean that a price increase is not possible at all. We can improve the odds of success by means of rigorous planning and execution.

5.4.1 Rob's Price Increase Campaign: A Fictitious Case

Rob is the Sales VP at one of the leading building materials companies in the country. He just got off the phone with the CFO, who gave him a price increase target. It was not news to Rob that almost all costs were on the rise, labor costs, energy costs, and raw materials. However, he did not know that the situation was already so precarious. The CFO told him that the company had exhausted all cost saving possibilities and had to increase the price by 10% on average. Otherwise, the company would soon be caught up in a liquidity crisis.

Rob let out a sigh. The company had not increased prices for at least 3 years. The competitors were always aggressive and eager to take market share from them. He had no idea how he was going to pull off the much-needed price increase. Nonetheless, he pulled out a piece of paper and began scribbling some numbers for himself.

As the company needed to see the cash inflow as soon as possible, Rob had to neglect those customers who had an annual supply contract for the price increase campaign. Prices for these customers are untouchable in the short run due to fixed-price agreements. As a result, the price increase target rose to 11%. See the starting situation in Table 5.4.

The annual revenue at that time was $300 million. Subtracting annual supply contracts, Rob was left with $280 million in revenue, which he could impact in the short-term, which translated into an effective price increase target of 11%.

Rob's gut feeling told himself that it would be exceedingly difficult to increase the price by 11% across the board. Then he recalled the customer ABCD analysis (see Table 5.2 to refresh your memory) he commissioned a few weeks ago. Maybe he could find some cues from there.

There was a total of 315 customers without annual supply contracts, of which 15 A customers contributed 50% of the revenue. Going through the customers in his mind, Rob tried to develop a feasible price increase target for each of the large customers. As there had been no price increases in the past 3 years, he figured it would be possible to enforce a 7% with the A customers which usually retained other suppliers at the same time. He could not recall the details of all B customers. However, he believed that a 12% price increase on average would be possible. He knew about only a very few C and D customers and had to double-check with his team. For the sake of a back-of-the-envelope calculation, it should be fine to assume a price increase targets of 14% and 15%, respectively. The results are summarized in Table 5.5.

Shoot, just 1% short of the price increase target. Where should he find the remaining $1.9 million? Furrowing his brow, he continued to work on the numbers. Suddenly, an idea struck him: how about further differentiate the price increase by product type? The revenue in scope could be split into sale of goods, which were commodity-like, and sale of

Table 5.4 Rob's price increase campaign—starting situation

Starting situation	
Annual revenue in k$	$300,000
Price increase target in %	10%
Price increase target in k$	$30,000
Revenue without annual supply contracts in k$	$280,000
Effective price increase in %	11%

Table 5.5 Rob's price increase campaign—price increase target by customer category

Category	#	Revenue share	Price increase target
A	15	50%	7%
B	50	25%	12%
C	100	20%	14%
D	150	5%	15%

Average price increase	10%
Price increase in k$	$28,140
Delta to target in k$	-$1,860

value-added services such as customized packaging, and rush orders. Customers were typically less price-sensitive to the latter, which were items off the radar. He examined the revenue shares by customer-product category and discovered that A and B customers used value-added services at a much higher proportion than C and D customers. In total, value-added services accounted for only 9% of total revenue. Rob decided to maintain the price increase target for goods while increasing the target for value-added services. Rob reasoned that because A customers would value value-added services more, he could set the price increase target for them at 20%. B and C customers could afford a 15% price increase for the value-added services. Let us see in Table 5.6 how the results improved.

Looking at the bottom line, the price increase campaign, in which the price targets were differentiated by customer and product, resulted in an average price increase of 11% on the revenue in scope. It translated into an additional revenue of slightly over the $30 million price increase target. Rob heaved a euphoric sigh of relief: it might work after all!

Rob dashed out the door to convene an emergency meeting with the sales leadership team. Rob reflected that it was a good start. However, there is still a lot of work to be done to make it happen.

Later. Rob returned to his office, deep in thought. Perhaps he was getting ahead of himself. Rob's passionate speech about his idea for the price increase campaign received a lukewarm response in the meeting room.

Table 5.6 Rob's price increase campaign—price increase target by customer-product category

Category	Revenue share		Price increase target	
	Goods	Value-added services	Goods	Value-added services
A	45%	5%	7%	20%
B	22%	3%	12%	15%
C	19%	1%	14%	15%
D	5%	0%	15%	0%

Average price increase	11%
Price increase in k$	$30,240
Delta to target in k$	$240

Rob took down the team's questions and promised to get back to them the next day with a proper response.

Some of the most critical questions read:

1. How did you account for lost sales in your calculation?
2. What do we do if our competitors take this opportunity to steal customers from us?
3. Most of the sales managers have never experienced an inflationary environment in their entire career. How can we prepare them for the price increase campaign?
4. What is Plan B should the plan not work out?

He had some ideas for how to approach these questions. He would, however, like to give them some thought. He would have to persuade the team the next time. If he could not persuade them, the price increase campaign would fail. Rob stayed late in the office that day and was seen talking on the phone for a long time.

The next morning Rob summoned another team meeting and responded to the abovementioned questions.

1. How did you account for lost sales in your calculation?

   I was assuming that we could get away with barely any lost sales. If we are well prepared and communicate the price increases properly, I think it is a realistic assumption. However, I agree that there might be a few shaky cases, especially concerning some of the A customers, which we need to examine in greater detail before taking actions with them. In the worst-case scenario, we would have to go for a lower price increase or grandfather them for a certain period.

2. What do we do if our competitors take this opportunity to steal customers from us?

   I guess it is an attempting thought for our competitors to keep their prices unchanged or even lower their prices to steal market share from us. However, having spoken to our colleagues and some experts in the industry, I consider it a rather unlikely scenario. Like us, all our major competitors have been experiencing painful cost explosions in recent years.

   In fact, because our facilities have been nearly fully depreciated, we may even have a cost advantage. Because our competitors have recently invested in new product lines, they are under even greater pressure to raise prices than we are.

   Not to mention that we are the market leader! If we raise our prices, our competitors will almost certainly follow suit. If some competitors do attack us, we will retaliate by getting at their most important customers.

3. Most sales managers have never experienced an inflationary environment in their careers. How can we prepare them for the price increase campaign?

   I admit that I overlooked this issue. It is a valid challenge that we need to work on before we launch the price increase campaign. I propose the following:

   (a) We need to draft a price increase guide, which lists the key actions, the rationale for an immediate price increase, counterarguments for complaints, etc.
   (b) We will organize a best practice sharing seminar, having sales veterans share their experience in how to sell price increases to customers and some practical tips.

(c) I suggest that we investigate with the HR department the possibility of introducing a special bonus linked to the success rate of the price increases to incentivize the sales team.

(d) We will form a Special Forces Unit consisting of the most experienced salespeople and management to provide support in difficult cases.

4. What is Plan B should the plan not work out?

   I am afraid we cannot afford to have a Plan B. We need to win this campaign together. Our company's fate is on the line. We must unite and find a solution. Frankly speaking, I am less concerned with C and D customers. It is critical to ensure our success rate with the big guys. I am determined to see through the enforcement of the price increases.

   I will personally stand behind taking extraordinary measures such as rejecting any customization requests, reducing support level, and even stopping supplies if it is necessary to implement the required price increases.

Rob's concluding remark in the meeting was decisive:

Last night, I gave it a lot of thought. We believe we are suppliers, and we have less bargaining power against our customers. It is not true.

We are in the same boat. Our customers and we are partners. If we fail, they fail. If we succeed in bringing this across, they will understand and accept it [the price increase]. They are otherwise in the wrong boat.

Soon after that meeting, the price increase campaign was officially kicked off with the blessing of the CEO of the company.

5.4.2 A Recapitulation

We did not know how Rob's price increase campaign turned out. However, it looked like a good plan. As the saying goes, good planning is half the battle. Let us recap the key steps that led up to Rob's price increase campaign.

Step 1: Determine the Overall Target
- Define revenue and customers in scope. Given the urgency, only customers without annual supply contracts were considered for the price increase campaign.
- The price increase target in absolute terms remained unchanged at $30 million, while the target in percentage rose to 11% after adjustment for revenue in scope.

Step 2: Break Down the Price Increase Target
- Categorize customers based on the insights from the ABCD analysis. Assign different targets for different customer categories, starting with the lowest target at 7% for A customers, rising for smaller customers, and ending at 15% for D customers.
The rationale: larger customers are more resourceful and have stronger negotiation power, while smaller customers are more dependent on suppliers and, as such, in a weaker position in price negotiations.
Realizing there was a gap to the price increase target

- Explore opportunities in further price differentiation by product type: keeping price increase target for the goods intact, increasing the target for the value-added services.
The rationale: there was more attention to the goods than to the value-added services. It can also be attributed to a psychological effect called mental accounting, a tendency of human beings to mentally assign funds to different pockets, for which the willingness to pay differs. The concept and implications of mental accounting will be explained in greater detail in Sect. 5.7.

Realizing that the planned measures could meet the price increase target

Step 3: Prepare for the Execution
- Socialize the price increase plan internally and collect feedback, especially from the sales managers who have firsthand information about the customers and the competitors.
- Sanity-check assumptions and feasibility, especially with respect to possible reactions of customers and competitors.

- Conduct a thorough examination of the most important customers and competitors, and plan ahead of time to ensure that everything is under control.
- Make sure adequate communication about the upcoming price increase campaign both internally and externally.
- Prepare a price increase guide for the sales team.
- Conduct training for the sales team to prepare them for possible reactions from customers and competitors when the price increase is announced.
- Provide the sales team with incentives linked to the success rate of the price increases.
- Have a Plan B! It is fine even if Plan B turns out to be Plan A after all.
- Finally, secure top management's blessing.

5.4.3 The Sequel

The other half of the battle still needs to be battled, obviously. I will highlight the key steps that should follow once a price increase campaign has been launched. For the sake of continuation, I follow the numbering mentioned above in the recapitulation.

Step 4: Prelaunch
- Rehearse communications and negotiations with the customers thoroughly within the team, both in writing and verbally. Conduct role plays or mock dialogs if necessary.
- If budget permits, run PR campaigns on the grave difficulties that the entire industry is facing, hinting at the pressing need for an immediate price increase. (*Do Not* talk to competitors directly. Price fixing is illegal and may face severe consequences in most countries.)
- Sales managers reach out to their respective customers and warm them up for the eventual arrival of "bad news"—it is especially important when the timing of the price increase campaign is close to the budgeting period of the customers.

Should reds flag be spotted at Step 4, it would be good to revisit Step 3 before launching. If else, proceed to the next step

Step 5: Break the News
– It is time to break the news. It should be a formal letter of price increase announcement signed by the Head of Sales or even a C-level executive if it is an important customer. The letter should include the following content: rationale of the unavoidable price increase, the magnitude of the price increase and timing, contact information of the person who oversees the communication in this matter. The more solid the fact base is, the less vulnerable you will be in the upcoming negotiations.
– Monitor closely and ensure full transparency on the progress.
– Take actions if there is remarkable deviation from the target.
– Celebrate successful cases, move on, and do not look back.

5.4.4 Last Remarks on Price Increase

A price increase is an unpleasant act for customers because it breaks the old balance. It can be unpleasant for your own salespeople for the very same reason. However, price increase campaigns should belong to the survival kit of every company.

A price increase is imperative as in Rob's case. The cost rocketed through the roof. No stone should be left unturned. It would be a shame if price, the No. 1 important profit level, did not play a role in this urgent mission. Rob's case shows that launching a successful price increase campaign can be a very tedious process under extremely high time pressure. Although the preparation is painful, the processes, guidelines, and learnings can be reused in the future. The efforts to design a proper price increase campaign will pay off. It is better to plan carefully than to rush recklessly despite the time pressure.

That said, we do not always have the luck and time to prepare everything neatly, have the perfect solution for every possible situation. With the time value of pricing measures (see Fig. 2.1) in mind, doing something in the right way is a better option than doing nothing. A pragmatic, top-down approach, such as the one that Rob used, is recommended and should suffice most of the time.

5.5 Stay Away from a Price War!

5.5.1 Nobody Wins in the End

A price war breaks out when companies in a highly competitive market continuously lower prices to undercut each other to gain market share. Companies tend to start a price war impulsively and often underestimate the consequences. In retrospect, it is almost never a clever idea to start or engage in a price war.

Customers may be pleased to see a price war, as they are going to pay less for the same product or service. Well, they should enjoy while it lasts. Eventually, the quality of the "same" product or service will likely deteriorate, as the focus of the competition shifts from value to price. Recall the bitter confession of the CEO of the irrigation equipment manufacturer in Sect. 1.2.

A downward price spiral would pick up momentum faster than you thought and ended in a heated price war. Price war participants will soon find themselves in an unfortunate situation: price goes down, market share does not go up, and cash is being burned at an alerting pace.

There are only two likely outcomes of a price war.

1. *Both parties agree to a truce.*

A price war may start out with multiple companies attacking each other. As the war escalates, usually only two parties stick to it in the end. When they agree to cease fire, the war is ended or at least there will be peace for a certain time before they pick it up again.

What are the results of the war? The price level of the entire industry has decreased, while the market shares remain more or less the same as before. Meanwhile, the profitability of all parties drops significantly. Remember price is the most important profit lever? This is true for price increases and decreases. Assuming a 20% operating profit margin, all it takes is a merely 20% price cut to wipe out every cent of profit in no time—it is a sad testimony to the unworthiness of all war participants.

Do customers come out as the winners of a price war after all? It depends on the time horizon. As mentioned earlier, customers may benefit in the beginning. However, funds that could have been invested to create something more valuable and sustainable for customers in the long run were expensed for today's pleasure. I do not know whether it is good or bad for customers.

2. *One party claims victory.*

The party with the strongest financial muscles would eventually declare victory, meaning seizing more market share, while the others concede. However, the winner is walking on a thin line.

The winner must find a way to increase price to turn a profit. It is difficult because customers have been spoiled and take everyday low price for granted. At the same time, the winner must watch out for competitors closely in case they decide to come back and engage in a price war again. Should the winner gain too much market power, the monopoly-like market position would likely invite unwanted attention from the antitrust body. As you can see, behind the glory there is not much fun being a winner like this.

As a price war is won on price, the success is built on sand. There will always be another richer or crazier guy to come after you, launching one price war and another. Low price per se is not an effective economic moat.

The ride hailing market in China is a case in point. It is a never-ending story. Didi appeared to be the sole winner coming out of an extended, seemingly endless price war (2012–2021) against local rivals such as Yongche and Kuaiche and the industry pioneer Uber. However, following Didi's suspension from the app stores due to its clash with the Chinese authorities, second-tier ride-hailing companies took the opportunity to gain market share while raising funds to increase spends on marketing and promotions targeting both drivers and customers. Meituan launched a new ride-sharing app in July 2021, and within 2 months, it had rolled out to more than 200 cities. In September 2021, the B2C ride-sharing platform Caocao Travel announced the completion of an RMB3.8 billion ($560 million) Series B. The following month, another competitor T3 announced that it had received an RMB7.7 billion ($1.1 billion) Series A. These contenders used the cash to expand into new cities and offered incentives to attract drivers (LIU, 2023). Didi was dragged back to the inception 10 years ago almost overnight. Was it all a slumber?

The truth is that no one can truly win a price war. The winner that comes out of a price war may just look like a "winner."

5.5.2 Rethink Price War

If a price war is bad for everyone involved, why do companies wage a war in the first place? Is a price war inevitable? Was there a sound business logic behind every price war fought or was it just because of someone's ego? Recent development in the automotive industry can provide us with some food for thought.

The German Volkswagen Group has been the undisputed market leader in China for decades. Its dominance came to a halt in the first quarter of 2023. Warren Buffet-backed Chinese manufacturer BYD sold a total of 552,076 vehicles in the first 3 months in 2023 and thus surpassed both Volkswagen joint ventures combined to become the bestselling brand in China (Anderson, 2023).

The competition in the passenger car market already heated up in 2022, not only in China but also in the USA, as Tesla went on the offensive and slashed prices several times in response to weakened consumer sentiment in the aftermath of the COVID-19 pandemic. Despite the price cuts, Tesla's China-made vehicles fell 31% in sales volume in July from June, while BYD was able to register sales increases in the same period (Reuters, 2023a).

The pressure on Volkswagen in its most important market was mounting by the day, as uprising local players were enjoying greater success with electric vehicles than their Western rivals. Unlike in its home market of Europe, VW's ID Family had lagged local competition in China, which underlay VW's dethronement in the EV era.

In September 2023 Volkswagen's joint venture in China, FAW-VW, drastically cut prices on ID.4 to 145,900 CNY (the launch price was 193,900 CNY), which is equivalent to less than 20,000 EUR (Johnson, 2023). In Germany, the retail price of ID.4 started from approximately 40,000 EUR. It was not an isolated case, as other ID. Family members shared a similar fate. In the past, the same car model from the German carmaker would retail for a much higher price in China than in its domestic market. The sea change epitomizes not only a shift of power in sales numbers, but also a shift of taste deep down in consumers' mind. The "Made-in-Germany" halo is fading away and there will be no easy coming back.

Acknowledging and making peace with the new normal, Ralf Brandstaetter, member of the board of management at Volkswagen AG / CEO Volkswagen Passenger Car, commented on Volkswagen's new strategic direction in China in an interview in May 2023:

"Volkswagen is focusing on a sustainable business model. In concrete terms, this means that we will not participate in the discount battle at any price," he added, "Our market position is strong enough. For us, the focus is on profitability, not sales volume or market share."

Brandstaetter expects the Chinese car market to grow from its current 22 million to between 28 and 30 million by 2030. "If we achieve sales of more than 4 million vehicles in this environment in 2030, with corresponding profitability, which is a position we could very well live with," he said (Reuters, 2023b).

Amidst intensifying competition, Volkswagen bought nearly 5% of Chinese electric vehicle maker XPeng for $700 million and agreed on a strategic partnership to develop two new car models. The German group's Audi subsidiary also committed to collaborating more closely with its Chinese partner, SAIC Motor, one of the leading state-owned carmakers (He, 2023).

Volkswagen gives us an idea on how to flee from a cut-throat price war.

What is the most important lesson here? Actions speak louder than words. Take a closer look at the timeline, and you will realize that the Volkswagen joint venture slashed the price on ID.4 after the interview given by Brandstaetter.

It is extremely difficult to survive a price war unscathed. To not get caught in the first place or have the upper hand when a price war is inexorable, companies should strive to maintain a competitive edge through innovations and a unique value proposition for their customers.

5.6 Dynamic Pricing

Dynamic pricing is on every pricing practitioner's lips. It is an elephant in the room that one cannot look past. It can be a silver bullet in certain situations; however, it is not a cure-all. For most product managers and pricing practitioners, dynamic pricing does not and should not play a role in their work.

Dynamic pricing, also referred to as surge pricing, demand pricing, or time-based pricing, is a revenue management pricing strategy in which businesses set flexible prices for products or services based on current market demands. Businesses can change prices based on algorithms that consider competitor pricing, supply and demand, and other external factors in the market (Wikipedia, 2023b).

In fact, dynamic pricing is most relevant in the context of yield management, which concerns about selling the right product to the right customer at the right time for the right price (also known as the 4 Rs of dynamic pricing). There are three essential conditions for dynamic pricing to be applicable (Wikipedia, 2023j):

- There is a fixed number of products available for sale.
- The products sold are perishable. There is a time limit to selling the products, after which they become valueless.
- There are customers willing to pay a different price for using the same product or service.

It should be noted that dynamic pricing is sometimes associated with negative connotations such as price gouging and price discrimination. Uber, Didi, and even Coco-Cola have been caught in controversial incidents where they fell out with their users. Check out my book "*The Pricing Puzzle*" should you be interested to learn more details.

In fact, there are only a handful of industries that are suitable for dynamic pricing. The most prominent examples are travel (e.g., airlines, car rentals), hospitality & tourism (e.g., hotels, rental apartments), and e-retail platforms (notably pioneered by Amazon).

In recent years, I have seen numerous industrial companies being eager to jump on the bandwagon and claiming to make use of dynamic pricing. Well, they do not understand dynamic pricing. Dynamic pricing is too farfetched as a pricing approach for most industrial companies. In dynamic pricing, only the price varies in a dynamic way, while the underlying product or service stays the same. The price differentiation potential for industrial companies should principally stem from custom solutions based on a solid understanding of customer segments. It has nothing to do with dynamic pricing.

The initiation and ensuing maintenance of dynamic pricing is complicated and industry specific. Further elaboration would be beyond the scope of this pricing compass. It suffices to know for now that there is no universal plug-and-play dynamic pricing solution, as the requirements and target setting are individual and evolving over time. It is dangerous to entrust machine learning or artificial intelligence alone with your dynamic pricing algorithm. Neither product managers nor pricing practitioners should desire a pricing black box. The guiding principles of any pricing technique must come from human beings, although humans do err.

5.7 Monetize the Predictable

It is old news that humans are predictably irrational. Behavioral economics has found increasingly wide application in pricing, leading to the rise of the so-called behavioral pricing which exploits predictable patterns of consumers to achieve more desirable results for the seller.

5.7.1 Behavioral Pricing vs. Value Pricing

Behavioral pricing does not contradict or replace value pricing. The latter tells us about the should-be price to be charged; the former deals with how to charge to realize the full potential of the should-be price. Value pricing reveals the theoretical price ceiling; behavioral pricing is more experimental, which means every merchant can experiment with a bit of behavioral pricing in their way and determine what works out the best for them. You may find the following anecdote (Schwarzenegger, 2013) inspiring.

Two young Europeans were fresh off the boat and founded a construction company in California, USA. While soliciting business, one of them would make the measurements at a prospective job site in meters and centimeters and then show them to his colleague. The two of them would argue in German until the customer came over and asked what was going on.

"I do not get why he thinks this patio will cost $8,000," the one who took the measurements explained, pulling the customer aside. "Between you and me, I think we can build it for $7,000." After some discussion with the customer and a little more arguing in German, the customer accepted the $7000 offer.

The two immigrants built a promising business in this manner before one of them left to pursue another career path. The one who took the measurements at the job site was an avid bodybuilder named Arnold Schwarzenegger, later also known as the Terminator and the Governor of California.

I am not sure whether Schwarzenegger knew that he was applying a behavioral pricing trick. However, obviously he nailed it. In what follows, I will discuss some of the most important behavioral pricing tricks.

5.7.2 Four Behavioral Pricing Tricks

1. *Magic Nine*

    Price endings with 9 are everywhere in retail: $0.99, $1.99, $9.9, $19, $79, $129… There are many theories and experiments testifying to the spell of the Magic Nine, which achieves better sales than any nearby prices.

    The deal effect is one of the most common explanations, especially when it results in a difference in digits, e.g., $99 feels much better than

$100. $0.99 feels like it is almost free (it is not, otherwise Apple Music would not have been so successful.)

My favorite theory is this: price elasticity nears zero within a small price segment (see demand curve No. 3 in Fig. 4.3). It means if the fair price of a product is $95, you should probably aim higher at $99, and it would not incur any loss of sales volume. It is a 4% nearly risk-free price premium served on a silver platter.

If this is true, then using Magic Nine should be a dominant strategy. Some retailers would prefer endings of 8 or 7 rather than 9. In my opinion, there is no compelling business reason to do so. It is essentially throwing money away. Customers will probably not appreciate the gesture either.

I debated with myself multiple times about the superiority of Magic Nine over the years: is there a number that can out-sell nine? The answer was always no. Magic 9 trumps. It feels stupid somehow. However, it is the way it is.

P.S. I have deliberately used Magic Nine and Magic 9 interchangeably. This is not so obvious; however, it is also a pricing trick. If you want to draw customers' attention to the price, use numbers; if not, use letters (smaller fonts would have the same effect, alleviating the pain caused by the price tag).

2. *Mental accounting*

Mental accounting is a model of consumer behavior developed by Richard Thaler that describes the process whereby people code, categorize, and evaluate economic outcomes.

As Thaler puts it, "All organizations, from General Motors down to single person households, have explicit and/or implicit accounting systems. The accounting system often influences decisions in unexpected ways" (Thaler, 2008).

Many households have purposefully reduced their spending in the aftermath of COVID-19 due to economic adversity and uncertainty. Because they have different priorities, they would adjust their spending in different ways: for example, some would postpone their vacations abroad, while others would cancel their Netflix subscriptions, despite the fact that a cent spent is a cent spent—or, more formally, both expenditures draw on the same fungible resource (income).

Another example is how a disaggregated price in communication influences a customer's value perception, and thus the purchase decision. Consider the following scenario: there are two offers for the same flight itinerary. The total cost is the same, i.e., $100. However, the price structure differs. The first offer has a base price of $80 and a surcharge of $20, while the second offer has a base price of $20 and a surcharge of $80. The second offer would appear to be a better deal in the eyes of the beholder.

The example of the plane ticket may remind you of Rob's price increase campaign in Sect. 5.4. Humans tend to simplify things, including their thought processes. They require surrogates to conduct the act of simplification.

The base price in the air ticket and the price of the goods in Rob's case serve as surrogates for price perception, where the cognitive focus lies. By drawing greater attention to a pocket in which the customers feel less important/painful, travel agencies can actively manage the price perception and influence customers' purchase behavior. Moreover, some savvy travel agencies would show only the base prices in the search results page and display the surcharges at the next step in a separate page—creating another barrier for customers to drop out of the booking process—this is known as *loss aversion*.

3. *Loss aversion*

Loss aversion holds that we feel the pain of a loss more than we feel the upside of a gain. Kahneman and Tversky have suggested that losses can be twice as powerful, psychologically, as gains (Kahneman, 1992).

One prominent implication of loss aversion in pricing is the use of discount vs. surcharge. Discount is perceived to be a gain and surcharge a loss. Customers feel more acutely about paying a surcharge than being happy about receiving a discount. Take shipping fees in an e-commerce shop as an example. The merchant has two options to frame the shipping fee:

(a) We offer you a **$5** cash discount if your order totals at least **$100** today.
(b) **$5** shipping fee will apply unless your order totals at least **$100** today.

Which option works better to nudge customers to buy more? Most likely it will be option b. The shipping fee as a surcharge has an additional benefit for the merchant. It could reduce returns because the shipping fee will not be refunded in case of return. Therefore, when selling something, it is smarter to tell the potential buyer what they will miss out on if they do not purchase the product or service, rather than what they will gain. Take, Temu,[10] a rising e-commerce star, as another example. New users will be given a 120 EUR voucher that can only be used on items in a 10-min flash sale as soon as the registration is completed. In the meantime, a countdown timer will appear, heightening the fear of missing out (FOMO).

Loss aversion also offers a possible explanation for why free trials are so popular, especially in the digital product space. Apple Music, LinkedIn, Spotify and Co. typically offer nonpaying customers free trials of premium service, e.g., 1 month. Customers will be charged after the trial period ends if they do not/forget to cancel the trial in time. A good portion of trial customers would be converted into paying customers if they are happy with the features of the premium service.

4. *Anchoring*

Do you still remember the story of the young Arnold Schwarzenegger? Anchoring is more powerful than we usually think. Try and do this. Pour water in three bowls. Fill one bowl with cold water, the second with hot water (not too hot to burn your fingers later!), and the third with lukewarm water. Now stick one hand in the cold water and the other one in the hot water. Keep them there for 30 s or so. Now put both of your hands into the lukewarm bowl. One hand will feel the

---

[10] Temu is an online marketplace operated by the Chinese e-commerce company PDD Holdings Inc. and headquartered in Boston. It offers heavily discounted goods, which are mostly shipped to consumers directly from China (Wikipedia, 2023h).

water is warm, the other one that it is cold. It is about the contrast. The same principle applies to price. Nothing is cheap or expensive by itself but relative to something (Laja, 2023).

A physical anchor prevents a boat from drifting away from where the captain wants it to be. A price anchor pulls judgment on fair value/price in its direction. Therefore, it is usually smart to make the first offer in a negotiation.

However, there is a caveat. The go-first strategy is superior only if you possess an information parity or advantage over the counterpart. Too high an initial offer would blow off the deal right away. Too low an initial offer could cost you a fortune.

Thomas Edison had an invention that he thought would improve the telegraph machine. Therefore, he took his ideas to the Western Union Telegraph Company. When the Western Union asked him to name his price, his initial instinct was to shoot for the moon and ask for $2000. However, for some reason he stopped himself and said instead, "How about you make me an offer." The Western Union opened with $40,000! That was at least 20 times what he was going to ask (and is the equivalent of nearly $1 million in today's currency). He used this unexpected windfall to build a laboratory where he later created the phonograph and the electric light bulb (Galinsky & Schweitzer, 2015). The story tells us that if you are not sure what information is missing, it is better to wait and listen before naming the price.

In addition to negotiations, anchoring also comes into play in retail. On Amazon, you will find that the price information of many products consists of three parts: an is-price (e.g., $9), a was-price (e.g., $~~10~~, shown as a strikethrough price), and the corresponding discount, $1 in this case. The price constellation is intended to show customers the savings they can enjoy as they purchase the item at a discounted price. The assumption is that customers are more likely to buy a product when they feel they are obtaining a good deal.

Following the same logic, retailers can optimize the product lineup and nudge customers to buy a certain product. It can be realized with a Good, Better, and Best (GBB) structure. The Better option is the product that we want to sell. The Best option serves as a value anchor, which offers the highest value; however, it also comes at the highest price; the Good option serves as a decoy, which is cheaper; however, it is short of the expectation on desired value. In comparison, the Better option combines the best of the two worlds, offering the best value for money. Humans find peace of mind in the golden middle because they avoid extremes.

5.8 Summary

- As business expands, pricing is on a trajectory to get out of hand without proper maintenance.
- To get a sense of current price quality, I recommend an ABCD analysis (Fig. 5.1, Tables 5.1 and 5.2).
- For the sake of coherent price management, a systematic product categorization is needed, based on which different pricing rules should be applied (Fig. 5.2).
  - **Focus products** have the highest visibility in the market.
  - **Flagship products** carry something unique that your competitors are difficult to copy, be it a product feature, or simply aesthetic appeal.
  - **Longtail products** would receive least attention from all sides—customers, competitors, and you yourself.
- While promotions could still make sense in the B2C sector, it is generally a bad idea for industrial companies to engage in price promotions.
- Regardless of the goal, the ultimate criterion for evaluating a promotion should be whether it helps the company make more profit.
- To get the best out of promotions, we need to answer three questions:
  - **Who is eligible for promotions?** (Fig. 5.3)
  - **What products are suitable for promotions?** (Fig. 5.4)
  - **How to design effective promotions?** (Fig. 5.5)
- The debate over direct sales vs. third-party distribution has not yet been settled. A most likely scenario is that both sales models will continue to coexist in the near future.

- Pricing governance in trade manifests itself primarily in the form of terms and conditions. Caution is advised when retouching any legacy distributor pricing systems.
- The evolution of distribution pricing can unfold in three phases (Fig. 5.7)
  - **Good**: price band
  - **Better**: price matrix (Table 5.3)
  - **Best**: price waterfall (Fig. 5.8)
- Most manufacturers use both discounts and rebates to incentivize or reward their distributors.
- In practice, discounts usually make up a larger proportion than rebates in the overall distributor compensation package. The share and size of rebates are subject to the strategic goals of the company and may change over time.
- Price increases are unavoidable under circumstances, especially in an inflationary environment. We can improve the odds of success by means of rigorous planning and execution (Tables 5.4, 5.5 and 5.6).
- A price increase campaign consists of five steps.
  - Determine the overall target
  - Break down the price increase target
  - Prepare for the execution
  - Prelaunch
  - Break the news
- Efforts to design a proper price increase campaign will pay off. It is better to plan carefully than to rush recklessly despite the time pressure.
- A price war breaks out when companies in a highly competitive market continuously lower prices to undercut each other to gain market share.
- There are only two likely outcomes of a price war.
  - Both parties agree to a truce: there is no winner.
  - One party claims victory: the winner may just look like a "winner."

- It is almost impossible to survive a price war unscathed.
- Companies should strive to maintain a competitive edge through innovations and a unique value proposition for their customers to avoid a price war.
- Dynamic pricing does not and should not play a role for most product managers and pricing practitioners in their work.
- Dynamic pricing is most relevant in the context of yield management, which concerns about selling the right product to the right customer at the right time for the right price (the 4 Rs of dynamic pricing).
- Dynamic pricing is sometimes associated with negative connotations such as price gouging and price discriminations.
- Behavioral economics has found increasingly wide application in pricing, leading to the rise of the so-called behavioral pricing which exploits predictable patterns of consumers to achieve more desirable results for the seller.
- Behavioral pricing does not contradict or replace value pricing. The latter tells us about the should-be price to be charged. The former deals with how to charge to realize the full potential of the should-be price.
- There are four behavioral pricing tricks that you should know.
    - Magic Nine: price endings with 9 trump!
    - Mental accounting: different pockets of budget despite fungible income
    - Loss aversion: a bird in the hand is worth two in the bush.
    - Anchoring: the power of a reference point—seize the first mover advantage!

6

Embark on the Pricing Journey

Kazuo Inamori, the late Japanese philanthropist, entrepreneur, and founder of Kyocera and KDDI, left us with twelve management principles. The sixth principle reads (Kazuo, 2010):

> "Pricing is top management's responsibility — to find that one point where customers are happy and the company is most profitable."
> - *Kazuo Inamori*

Inamori asserted that "[pricing] is not the sales manager—let alone a salesperson—who should find that one point. Rather, it should be the responsibility of top management. This should be the universal principle for price setting."

My own experience confirms that companies with top management that prioritizes price management have strong pricing prowess, which translates into superior financial performance. The pricing journey is long and bumpy, which can be roughly divided into three major phases. See Fig. 6.1. The so-called pricing job should have different priorities in distinct phases.

Fig. 6.1 The three phases of a pricing journey

6.1 Set Sail

A promising business is forming at the outset. The founder is usually the product manager at the same time, who is bootstrapping almost everything. Among everything, there is one thing of utmost importance. It is to validate the product-market-price fit (see Figs. 3.1 and 3.2 in Chap. 3).

The price or the willingness to pay of the target customers is the ultimate yardstick of the feasibility of a fledgling business idea. At this stage, the founder is also the pricing captain, who should focus on the following questions about pricing:

1. Do I have a valid value proposition for my target customers?
2. What is the price that they are willing to pay?
3. What pricing model would fit the new business idea?
4. Is there a valid business case?

If there is mismatch between perceived value, price, and cost, the business plan needs to be revised or even disregarded. The founder, more than anyone else, should spend sufficient time surveying potential customers directly, not only to understand how the new product is going to add value for them, but also to have a feel of how much the customers are willing to pay for it. Although the initial indications from the interactions with these potential customers need to be substantiated as described in Chap. 3, the firsthand insights will already help a great deal to calibrate the value/price positioning of the new product.

According to my observation, startup founders who have zest for pricing stand out from the rest in that they excel at articulating what their business is about in brief and have a clear idea of how to win over customers. My theory is that those who appreciate pricing are conscious about creating something unique for customers instead of just copying others' success models. To perfect a product, the price as an integral part of the product concept needs to be perfect too. The very fact that the founder undertakes the pricing job her/himself is sending a strong signal to the entire team: pricing is an important matter to the company.

Given the importance of pricing, pricing cannot be a one-man job; given the complexity of pricing that accompanies the business growth, pricing needs to be managed by a dedicated team. If the company survives the early days, it is time for the founder to pass on the part of operative pricing to a pricing manager, a role that can be stepped up to the pricing director to keep abreast of the organizational growth at a later point. However, the founder or CEO should retain oversight of the pricing strategy, as Kazuo Inamori pleaded.

6.2 Navigate Rough Waters

As the business prospers and proliferates, pricing becomes increasingly complicated. Chapter 4 provides some insights into the typical challenges that stem from the customers. Diversification of the customer base calls for product and price differentiation. Differentiation is inevitably paralleled by complexity, which is compounded by various working threads that arise over time.

The pricing manager should be a master of many things: business intelligence, data analysis, costing, demand forecasting, market research, customer profiling, financial modeling, and project management.

The pricing manager should own the pricing process, including initial pricing for new products, pricing maintenance (market intelligence, competitive benchmarking, data mining, price monitoring and reporting, etc.), special price approvals (guidelines for price escalation, deal approvals), promotion management (design and execution), price optimization (regular price adjustment, contingent price increase/decrease campaigns, portfolio rationalization, etc.), and so on.

Experience shows that pricing maintenance alone can easily consume over 80% of the time of a pricing manager in a large organization. Many pricing managers that I know of would describe their job as a mind-numbing treadmill—deadly for a job of strategic and analytical nature.

Unfortunately, the pricing job is often thankless. To perform their duties, pricing managers must heavily rely on virtually all functions in the organization—sales, marketing, procurement, finance, strategy, and all the way to top management—to effect change. However, the incentive for cross-functional cooperation is often absent. At times, there are even conflicts between departments, especially with the sales team.

The sales team is cheered as a revenue-generating unit. The pricing team, on the other hand, is regarded as a supportive function. The Head of Sales usually outranks the pricing manager or whoever heads the pricing function. It is not hard to imagine how much pressure the pricing manager must cope with when she or he must disapprove of a special price request submitted by a top seller. Things can become uncomfortable very soon. Compromises will be made.

There will also be heated discussions with, for example, the finance controller, who would demand at least 20% gross margin for the new product, which would translate into a retail price that would shoot oneself in the foot. In the end, compromises will be made again. The list of compromises goes on.

Many pricing managers struggle at work. In fact, they are hierarchically ill-equipped to own the pricing process. With all due respect, what is expected of them is above their pay grade. This is especially true in organizations, where the CEO just newly found the importance of pricing and decided to hire someone outside the organization to form and lead a pricing team. It would be miraculous if it worked. Pricing is so intertwined with other functions that an outsider with neither prior knowledge nor political prowess will not be able to move the needle.

Even though it is a wonderful thing to have the founder or CEO as the guardian angel alongside, they cannot babysit the pricing manager or even the pricing director all the time. It does not help either to facelift the job title to *strategic pricing manager*, *strategic pricing director*, or the like. You see the CEOs themselves do not need the word "*strategic*" in their title to do their job. The longer the title, the less the real power there is.

To tap the full pricing potential, the pricing function needs to be headed by someone who has a seat at the table in the C-suite. There is an increasing number of companies going in this direction. Due to its versatile nature, the supreme commander of pricing should not be entitled the chief pricing officer (CPO). More often, we encounter executives carrying the title Chief Revenue Officer (CRO) or, more recently, Chief Growth Officer (CGO), whose mandate includes pricing as a key component. I personally prefer the notion of CGO, as it alludes to the essence of pricing—a beacon of hope for better growth.

6.3   Sail to New Shores

The new CGO has finally assumed office, paving the way for an end-to-end value creation and pricing process. In addition to safeguarding proper design and execution of pricing rules, all that has to do with the operative, short-term side of pricing, the CGO is also tasked with steering future growth of the company in the longer term. Their typical work scope would include, for example:

- Analyze and prioritize potential growth routes for the next 5–10 years.
- Devise a blueprint for future growth strategy that spans multiple dimensions, e.g., customer, innovation, geography, etc.
- Form and lead special growth squads across distinct functions to penetrate and expand in new markets.
- Provide guidance on the brand and marketing strategy of new businesses in alignment with the current business.

Pricing is ubiquitous even if it does not appear at all in the work scope above. CGOs are comparable to founders of corporate startups. No wonder their vision and responsibilities remind of what a founder is supposed to do at the outset (see Chap. 3). In this context, value-based pricing is a useful tool to fathom unchartered waters in the hope of discovering a new blue ocean.

6.4 Per Astra Ad Astra

It was a sunny afternoon. I was sitting in microeconomics class, listening to a lecture about market structures, supply and demand, implications on pricing, and of course of a bunch of puzzling formulas and graphs.

There was this important concept called *perfect competition*. Companies are said to be in perfect competition when the following conditions are met (Google Classroom, 2023):

- Many companies produce **identical products**.
- **Many buyers** are available to buy the product, and **many sellers** are available to sell the product.
- Sellers and buyers have **all relevant information** to make **rational decisions** about the product being bought and sold.
- Companies can enter and leave the market without any restrictions—in other words, there is **free entry and exit** into and out of the market.

A perfectly competitive company is known as a *price taker* because the pressure of competing companies forces them to accept the prevailing equilibrium price in the market. If a company in a perfectly competitive market raises the price of its product by so much as a penny, it will lose all its sales to competitors. The *market price* is determined solely by supply and demand in the entire market.

I have always found microeconomics intriguing: it is abstract and beautiful. According to French philosopher Simone Weil, "*Distance is the soul of the beautiful.*" Only through a distance, in space or in time, does reality undergo purification (Haven, 2012). The perfect competition described in the textbook is not what we live. The same also applies to the other extreme, i.e., monopoly, representative of an utterly imperfect competition, in which a single seller assumes a dominant position. The monopolist is, in contrast to a perfectly competitive company, a *price setter*, although antitrust legislation goes to great lengths to restrict monopolies to protect customers. Extremes are rare, whereas in-betweens are more common. As a result, most businesses are caught between price takers and price setters most of the time.

However, who wants to be a price taker? No, every company should strive to be a price setter. Price takers are at the mercy of the others. A perfect competition is not perfect for the customers from a long-term perspective, because the implicit price that they must pay for the fair market price is a lack of means to finance innovations for the next big thing.

Price setters such as Apple, Google, Huawei, Nvidia, Tesla and Co. are trend setters in their respective fields. Their pricing power is rooted in their dedication to innovations. Their pricing power would also dwindle between blockbusters. The time window in which to enjoy great freedom in setting prices is precious.

It is time to act. Carpe diem!

6.5 Summary

- Pricing is top management's responsibility—to find that one point where customers are happy, and the company is most profitable.
- The long pricing journey comprises three phases (Fig. 6.1).

    - **Set sail**: the founder is the product manager and pricing captain.
    - **Navigate rough waters**: a dedicated pricing force is formed, while the founder/CEO retains oversight of the pricing strategy.
    - **Sail to new shores**: the pricing role is elevated, as the Chief Growth Officer (CGO) assumes office and takes charge of exploring new opportunities.

- Price takers are doomed. Let us strive to be price setters. Act now!

References

Aesthetics Wiki. (2023, September). *Techwear*. Retrieved from Aesthetics Wiki: https://aesthetics.fandom.com/wiki/Techwear

Amazon. (2023, September 29). *How to get started?* Retrieved from Amazon.com: https://www.amazon.com/b/ref=s9_acss_bw_cg_SSFNAV21_2c1_w?&node=15283820011&pf_rd_m=ATVPDKIKX0DER&pf_rd_s=merchandised-search-3&pf_rd_r=WW8GS02G9SDWAP9Y787Y&pf_rd_t=101&pf_rd_p=6c99a94e-2490-45c4-93a8-88505267f4fc&pf_rd_i=5856181011

Anderson, B. (2023, June 1). *VW won't engage in a price war in China, focuses on profitability instead*. Retrieved from carscoops.com: https://www.carscoops.com/2023/06/vw-wont-engage-in-a-price-war-in-china-focuses-on-profitability-instead/

Barkley, A. (2023, September). *Marginal revenue and the elasticity of demand*. Retrieved from socialsci.libretexts.org: https://socialsci.libretexts.org/Bookshelves/Economics/The_Economics_of_Food_and_Agricultural_Markets_(Barkley)/03%3A_Monopoly_and_Market_Power/3.03%3A_Marginal_Revenue_and_the_Elasticity_of_Demand

Curling-Hope, L. (2022, July 12). *An introduction to Amazon pricing in 2022*. Retrieved from omniaretail.com: https://www.omniaretail.com/blog/an-introduction-to-amazon-pricing#:~:text=Amazon%20price%20 changes&text=The%20company%20is%20a%20pioneer,and%20consumers%20to%20keep%20up

Dupuit, J. (1849). *On tolls and transport charges.* Macmillan.

Evans, M. (2021, November 18). *The 4 essential types of consumer profiling.* Retrieved from Attest: https://www.askattest.com/blog/videos/the-4-essential-types-of-consumer-profiling

Galinsky, A., & Schweitzer, M. (2015). *Friend & foe: When to cooperate, when to compete, and how to succeed at both.* Currency. Retrieved from Fast Company: https://www.fastcompany.com/3054022/when-to-make-the-first-offer-in-a-negotiation-according-to-science

Google Classroom. (2023, October). *Perfect competition and why it matters.* Retrieved from Khan Academy: https://www.khanacademy.org/economics-finance-domain/microeconomics/perfect-competition-topic/perfect-competition/a/perfect-competition-and-why-it-matters-cnx

Hanlon, A. (2023, March 20). *The AIDA model.* Retrieved from Smart Insights: https://www.smartinsights.com/traffic-building-strategy/offer-and-message-development/aida-model/

Haven, C. L. (2012). *"Distance is the soul of beauty." Finally. He explains.* Retrieved from The Book Haven: https://bookhaven.stanford.edu/2012/08/distance-is-the-soul-of-beauty/#:~:text=offers%20this%20elucidation%3A-,%E2%80%A6,time%2C%20does%20reality%20undergo%20purification

He, L. (2023, July 27). *Volkswagen invests $700 million in Chinese EV maker Xpeng to boost sluggish sales.* Retrieved from CNN Business: https://edition.cnn.com/2023/07/27/cars/china-volkswagen-xpeng-investment-intl-hnk/index.html

Hoover, G. (2022, December 2). *Peter Drucker on business purpose, tasks, profit, and social responsibility.* Retrieved from profectusmag: https://profectusmag.com/peter-drucker-on-business-purpose-tasks-profit-and-social-responsibility/

Johnson, P. (2023, September 4). *Volkswagen slashes ID.4 prices in China, now starting at $20,000.* Retrieved from electrek: https://electrek.co/2023/09/04/volkswagen-slashes-id-4-prices-china-starting-20000/

Kahneman, D. (1992). Advances in prospect theory: Cumulative representation of uncertainty. *Journal of Risk and Uncertainty, 5*(4), 297–323. https://doi.org/10.1007/BF00122574

Kazuo, I. (2010, October 31). *What are the twelve management principles?—6. Pricing is management.* Retrieved from Kyocera: https://global.kyocera.com/inamori/management/twelve/twelve06.html

Kundu, K. (2018, January 19). *Apple reportedly cutting distributor margins to end online discounts in India.* Retrieved from Beebom.com: https://beebom.com/apple-cutting-distributor-margins-end-online-discounts-india/

Laja, P. (2023, August 3). *Pricing experiments you might not know, but can learn from.* Retrieved from cxl.com: https://cxl.com/blog/pricing-experiments-you-might-not-know-but-can-learn-from/

Liu, T. W. (2023, February 14). *Didi's revival shows China can't live without big tech.* Retrieved from wired.co.uk: https://www.wired.co.uk/article/didis-revival-shows-china-cant-live-without-big-tech#:~:text=Didi%20was%20founded%20as%20Didi,China's%20biggest%20tech%20companies%2C%20Alibaba

Mueller, K. (2021, September 20). *This is why Pringles aren't really potato chips.* Retrieved from Reader's Digest: https://www.rd.com/article/are-pringles-potato-chips/

Nesbit, J. (2023, April 17). *Costco's Kirkland Signature Brand is wildly popular—But why?* Retrieved from yahoo!finance: https://finance.yahoo.com/news/costco-evolution-kirkland-signature-brand-155446969.html#:~:text=By%201995%2C%20the%20private%20brand,other%20cost%20efficiencies%2C%20per%20CNN

Optimove. (2023, September). *Customer acquisition and customer retention.* Retrieved from Optimove: https://www.optimove.com/resources/learning-center/customer-acquisition-vs-retention-costs

Pfeifer, A. (2019, January 21). *How to run studies using the Kano method.* Retrieved from usertimes: https://usertimes.io/2019/01/21/how-to-run-studies-using-the-kano-method/#:~:text=The%20standardized%20Kano%20questionnaire%20proposes,lacks%20the%20feature%20in%20question

Randall, C. (2021, May 21). *Volkswagen to apply agency sales model to group brands.* Retrieved from electrive.com: https://www.electrive.com/2021/05/21/vw-to-apply-agency-model-to-group-brands/

Ray, J. (2019, December 13). *Warren Buffett on pricing power and your idiot nephew.* Retrieved from Ray Business Advisors: https://www.raybusinessadvisors.com/warren-buffett-on-pricing-power-and-your-idiot-nephew/#:~:text=If%20you've%20got%20the,look%20at%20it%20in%20context

Reuters. (2023a, August 14). *Tesla cuts prices in China for select Model Y versions*. Retrieved from Reuters: https://www.reuters.com/business/autos-transportation/tesla-cuts-prices-china-some-model-y-versions-2023-08-14/#:~:text=Tesla%20reduced%20the%20starting%20prices,349%2C900%20yuan%2C%20down%203.8%25

Reuters. (2023b, May 31). *Volkswagen won't join China discount battle "at any price," COO says*. Retrieved from Reuters: https://www.reuters.com/business/autos-transportation/volkswagen-wont-participate-china-discount-battle-any-price-coo-2023-05-31/

Schwarzenegger, A. (2013). *Total recall: My unbelievably true life story*. Simon & Schuster.

Sheldon, R. (2022, September). *Unique selling point (USP)*. Retrieved from techtarget.com: https://www.techtarget.com/whatis/definition/unique-selling-point-USP

Simon, H. (2015). *Confessions of the pricing man*. Copernicus.

Simon, H. (2021). *True profit!*. Copernicus.

Slater, D. (2023). *The imperatives of customer-centric innovation*. Retrieved from aws: https://aws.amazon.com/executive-insights/content/the-imperatives-of-customer-centric-innovation/

Stobierski, T. (2020, December 12). *What is conjoint analysis, and how can it be used?* Retrieved from Harvard Business School Online: https://online.hbs.edu/blog/post/what-is-conjoint-analysis#:~:text=Conjoint%20analysis%20works%20by%20asking,to%20develop%20its%20pricing%20strategy

Thaler, R. (2008). Mental accounting and consumer choice. *Marketing Science, 27*, 15–25. https://doi.org/10.1287/mksc.1070.0330

Wallstreetmojo Team. (2023). *Market price*. Retrieved from Wallstreetmojo: https://www.wallstreetmojo.com/market-price/

Wikipedia. (2023a, September). *Conjoint analysis*. Retrieved from Wikipedia: https://en.wikipedia.org/wiki/Conjoint_analysis

Wikipedia. (2023b, October 4). *Dynamic pricing*. Retrieved from Wikipedia: https://en.wikipedia.org/wiki/Dynamic_pricing

Wikipedia. (2023c, September). *Gabor–Granger method*. Retrieved from Wikipedia: https://en.wikipedia.org/wiki/Gabor%E2%80%93Granger_method

Wikipedia. (2023d, September). *Gross merchandise volume*. Retrieved from Wikipedia: https://en.wikipedia.org/wiki/Gross_merchandise_volume

Wikipedia. (2023e). *Kano model*. Retrieved from Wikipedia: https://en.wikipedia.org/wiki/Kano_model

Wikipedia. (2023f, September). *KISS principle*. Retrieved from Wikipedia: https://en.wikipedia.org/wiki/KISS_principle

Wikipedia. (2023g, September). *Loss leader*. Retrieved from Wikipedia: https://en.wikipedia.org/wiki/Loss_leader

Wikipedia. (2023h, November 1). *Temu (marketplace)*. Retrieved from Wikipedia: https://en.wikipedia.org/wiki/Temu_(marketplace)

Wikipedia. (2023i, September). *Van Westendorp's price sensitivity meter*. Retrieved from Wikipedia: https://en.wikipedia.org/wiki/Van_Westendorp%27s_Price_Sensitivity_Meter

Wikipedia. (2023j, October 4). *Yield management*. Retrieved from Wikipedia: https://en.wikipedia.org/wiki/Yield_management

Yahoo Finance. (2023, September 29). *Yahoo Finance*. Retrieved from Yahoo Finance: https://finance.yahoo.com/

Yang, J. Y. (2020). *The pricing puzzle*. Springer. https://doi.org/10.1007/978-3-030-50777-0_12

Zhang, P. (2023, September 11). *Xpeng to gradually replace direct stores with dealers, report says*. Retrieved from cnevpost.com: https://cnevpost.com/2023/09/11/xpeng-to-replace-direct-stores-with-dealers-report/

Index

A
Aldi, 59
Alibaba, 90
Amazon, 81, 92, 93
Android, 98
Apple, 98, 103, 121, 123, 135
Apple Music, 121, 123

B
Bezos, J., 21
Black Friday, 90
BYD, 116

C
Caocao, 115
Coco-Cola, 118
Conjoint, 10, 38–40

Costco, 51, 60
COVID-19, 116

D
Didi, 115
Double 11, 90, 91
Drucker, P., 21
Duhigg, C., 93

E
Ebay, 46
Edison, T., 124

F
Frey, E., 95

Index

G
Gabor Granger, 35–38, 42
General Motors, 94, 121
Google, 135
Green, P.E., 38

H
Huawei, 135

I
Instafloss, 44–46

K
KANO model, 24, 26, 62
Kickstarter, 44, 46
Kirkland Signature, 60
KISS principle, 90
Kuaiche, 115

L
Lego, 6
Li Auto, 94
Lidl, 86, 87
LinkedIn, 123

M
McDonald's, 63
Michelin, 60

N
Netflix, 121
Nio, 94
Nvidia, 135

P
PDD, 123n10
Power of Habit, 93
Price elasticity, 65–74
Pricing sandbox, 29, 31
Product-market fit, 22
Product-market-price fit, 22–24, 77

S
Schwarzenegger, A., 120
Simon, H., 22
618, 91
Spotify, 123

T
Temu, 123, 123n10
Tesla, 59, 94, 116, 135
Thaler, R., 121
Toyota, 94
T3, 116

U
USP, 24–28, 47, 49

V

van Westendorp, 31–35, 37
Volkswagen, 94, 116

W

Weil, S., 134
Western Union, 124

X

Xpeng, 94

Y

Yongche, 115

GPSR Compliance
The European Union's (EU) General Product Safety Regulation (GPSR) is a set of rules that requires consumer products to be safe and our obligations to ensure this.

If you have any concerns about our products, you can contact us on

ProductSafety@springernature.com

In case Publisher is established outside the EU, the EU authorized representative is:

Springer Nature Customer Service Center GmbH
Europaplatz 3
69115 Heidelberg, Germany

www.ingramcontent.com/pod-product-compliance
Lightning Source LLC
LaVergne TN
LVHW010959250326
834688LV00003B/14